# FLASHBACK

A Pictorial History 1879-1979
One hundred years of Stratford-upon-Avon
and the Royal Shakespeare Company

# FLASHBACK

A Pictorial History 1879-1979
One hundred years of Stratford-upon-Avon
and the Royal Shakespeare Company

**by Micheline Steinberg**

RSC Publications
1985

© Royal Shakespeare Theatre and Micheline Steinberg
1985

ISBN 0 9505057 7 3

**Designed by Richard Fuller**

**Cover pictures:** Vivien Leigh (Lady Macbeth), 1955, *photo: Angus McBean.*
Frank Benson (Macbeth), c 1905-1906 *photo: Beagles.*
Ian McKellen and Judi Dench (Macbeth and Lady Macbeth), 1976, *photo: Joe Cocks.*

**Title page pictures:** *(right)* Alan Howard as Jack Rover in *Wild Oats* (1976) by John O'Keeffe at
the Aldwych Theatre, *photo: Reg Wilson;* and *(left)* the same role played by his great-grandfather,
Edward Compton at the Shakespeare Memorial Theatre in Stratford-upon-Avon in 1882.

Published by RSC Publications
Phototypesetting and artwork production by Oxglen Services Ltd (IGDS), London
Litho origination by Lithocraft Ltd., Coventry
Printed by the Herald Press, Stratford-upon-Avon

# CONTENTS

# ACKNOWLEDGEMENTS

How do you judge your success when you attempt the impossible? The impossible task of this book is to capture, in just over a hundred pages, just over a hundred years of theatre. And so I appear like the Chorus in *Henry V*, begging my audience to, "Piece out our imperfections with your thoughts". The armies this book sets out to represent are not of soldiers, though, but of actors, directors, designers and all those who worked on or behind or in front of the stage, playing their part in the history of what is now known as the Royal Shakespeare Company. To them this book is dedicated. It cannot hope to do them justice but may succeed in a more modest aim: of bringing some of the treasures of the Stratford theatre's archive to a wider audience.

I must thank Ellen Goodman (until recently the RSC's Publications Editor) for giving me the opportunity to. write this story, and her successor, Margaret Gaskin, for her editorial diligence; Dr Levi Fox for his permission to reproduce archival material from the Shakespeare Birthplace Trust and Marion Pringle, Mary White and Sylvia Morris at the Shakespeare Birthplace Trust Library, Stratford-upon-Avon, for their indefatigable assistance in checking facts and supplying information and photographs from the archives; Temo and Jacky for typesetting and artwork; Susan Pilgrim for her advice; and Robin Ellison whose intemperence and word processor made this book possible.

I am happy to thank all the personal contributors whose enthusiasm and encouragement provided me with much inspiration; I am only sorry that it has not been possible to include more than a few of their anecdotes and histories in this place.

Books consulted include: *Footnotes to the Theatre*, edited by R.D. Charques, Peter Davies 1938; *The Shakespeare Memorial Theatre* by Ruth Ellis, Winchester Publications, 1948; *Benson and The Bensonians* by J.C. Trewin, 1960; *Paul Scofield* by J.C. Trewin, 1956; *John Gielgud* by Ronald Hayman, Heinmanne 1971; *Edith Evans* by J.C. Trewin, 1954; *Limelight and After* by Claire Bloom, Weidenfeld and Nicolson, 1982; *Shakespeare Memorial Theatre, 1948-50, 1951-53, 1954-56. 1957-59*, Reinhardt and Evans; *Shakespeare's Histories at Stratford 1951*, J. Dover Wilson & T.C. Worsley, 1952; *Barry Sullivan and His Contemporaries*, London 1901; *Mainly Players*, Constance Benson, 1926; *The Royal Shakespeare Company, A History of Ten Decades* by Sally Beauman, OUP 1982; *Confessions of An Actor*, Laurence Olivier, Weidenfeld and Nicolson, 1982; *The Story of the Lyric Theatre Hammersmith*, Nigel Playfair, Chatto and Windus, 1925; *Myself and The Theatre* by Theodore Komisarjevsky, Heinemann; *First Interval* by Donald Wolfit; *A Bridges-Adams Letter Book* by Robert Speaight, The Society for Theatre Research 1971; *Richard Burton* by Paul Ferris, Weidenfeld and Nicolson, 1981; *Just Resting* by Leo McKern, Methuen (1983); *In My Mind's Eye* by Michael Redgrave, Weidenfeld and Nicolson 1983; *A Touch of The Memoirs* by Donald Sinden, Hodder and Stoughton 1982; *These Our Actors* by Richard Findlater, Elm Tree Books/Hamish Hamilton, 1983; *Helpmann* by Elizabeth Salter, Angus and Robertson 1978; *Godfrey, A Special Time Remembered* by Hodder and Stoughton 1983.

Newspaper quotations are derived largely from the Theatre Records of The Shakespeare Birthplace Trust.

Unless otherwise credited, photographs are from the collection of the Royal Shakespeare Theatre Collection, The Shakespeare Centre Library, Stratford-upon-Avon. That of Frank Benson as Richard II (1897), page 18, from the Mander and Mitchenson Collection; Tom Holte photographs are from the Tom Holte Theatre Photographic Collection.

Credits have, wherever possible, been given and consents obtained for reproduction of material, but it has not always proved possible in the case of older material. No lack of courtesy is intended by an omission, which will be remedied, if notified, in any future edition.

# FOREWORD

## DAME PEGGY ASHCROFT

"What do I remember?": a game we all can play who have visited the theatre at Stratford-upon-Avon — both during its existence as the Memorial and, in the last quarter of a century, as the Royal Shakespeare. Sally Beauman's wonderfully comprehensive history of the theatre has already textually indicated the changes and developments in style that have taken place within our lifetime. Now this volume of visual history, graphically illustrates those developments. And it will bring back to audiences and participators alike (and introduce to those who are too young to have known at first hand), just what it was like to experience one of the most astonishingly creative theatre companies of the century.

I look through the listed contents of this book and it revives\myriad memories; I close my eyes and summon up my own recollections of the most vivid of those memories in my mind's eye.

From the early thirties I pluck two that are as strong as anything that I can remember — Komisarjevsky's productions and designs for *The Merchant of Venice* and *King Lear* — in the former I can still see the Venetian Bridge dividing in the middle and Belmont rising up like a Tiepolo Vision with Portia (Fabia Drake) and her household. (I think this was the first use of the newly installed hydraulic lift.) In *Lear*, the opening of the play — a simple permanent set of a flight of steps, at the top of which sat Randle Ayrton, enthroned, a Blake-like, unforgettable Lear; on either side stood four Trumpeters raising their long trumpets in a fanfare in unison

with the rise of the curtain — the visual and musical effect of this was so striking that I think not one critic remarked that the opening scene of the play had been cut! (I neither commend nor criticise either of these facts)!

From the fifties I especially recall Peter Brook's dark production of *Titus Andronicus* — the figure of Vivien Leigh with fragments of red ribbons falling from her mutilated arms is particularly etched on my memory; more shocking than many realistically blood-bespattered horrors — and I see, like a triptych, on either side of her, Olivier's monumental Titus and the lithe powerful figure of Anthony Quayle's Aaron, fleeing with the baby in his arms.

From the sixties, few will forget the astonishing sensation of intense heat and disturbing beauty when Peter Hall's sand-pit for *Troilus and Cressida* was revealed; or the black menace of Trevor Nunn's and Christopher Morley's *The Revenger's Tragedy;* or in 1970, the world-acclaimed *A Midsummer Night's Dream*, Peter Brook's magical transformation.

Nearer to the present, two productions are fixed in my mind's eye — John Barton's *Love's Labour's Lost* designed by Ralph Koltai with its autumnal beauty and serenity, and Terry Hands' *Richard II* with Farrah's incandescent designs which engraved Alan Howard's amazing performance onto the perpetual retina of memory.

Of the exciting new developments at The Other Place — three personal recollections. Buzz Goodbody's production of *Hamlet* with Ben Kingsley, Trevor Nunn's definitive production of *Three Sisters* and Jane Lapotaire's searing performance in Howard Davies' production of Pam Gems' *Piaf*. But there are so many more which have to be the victims of a preface's limited space.

The actor has a different kind of physical memory — feeling rather than seeing the 'rightness' of his background. I cherish the memory of Margaret Harris's designs for Glen Byam Shaw's *Antony and Cleopatra* in 1953, with its economic but total expression of the rival essences of Rome and Egypt; the witty invention of Mariano Andreu's design for Gielgud's production of *Much Ado About Nothing*. In the sixties, *The Wars of the Roses* began a new era

with the bold and epic feeling that Peter Hall gave us with John Bury's threatening background, to be later developed throughout the history canon.

These are a few of many productions that we as actors have been enriched by — and that feeling of 'rightness' was crystallised for me in John Gunter's design for Trevor Nunn's *All's Well that Ends Well* where we entered a world we were all able to relate to and believe in — was it Shakespeare's world — or Chekhov's? No matter. In the world of *make* believe, actors and designers must be united.

I have limited my *'recalls'* mainly to the Stratford-based productions. After 1960, when Peter Hall's vision of a permanent company based on Stratford and London came into being, the explosion of work and number of productions, first in the two main theatres and later expanded into four auditoria became so prolific that the memory boggles. The productions ranged from John Whiting to David Edgar, taking in amongst many others: Aeschylus, Albee, Brecht, Chekhov, Duras, Euripedes, Feiffer, Gorki, Ibsen, Pinter, Sophocles and Strindberg — and four especially memorable ventures: Peter Brook's *Theatre of Cruelty;* John Barton's *The Greeks;* David Jones' productions of Gorki; and finally, Nunn's and Caird's nine-hour *Nicholas Nicklbey* — an experience without parallel in the theatre.

This huge development, in a little over 20 years, inaugurated by Peter Hall and then later carried on by Trevor Nunn (latterly with Terry Hands) — is chronicled photographically in this book and I invite you as readers to take up my memory game. As the RSC enters its second century, new directors are adding to its lustre. The excellence of their skills is sometimes said to lead the RSC into becoming a 'director's' theatre; I think, however, the actors' ready commitment to the work, if nothing else, gives the lie to this, and this book shows that nothing in recent years has changed that position. To have been a traveller on this voyage is the most memorable venture in my life.

I would like to end with a grateful acknowledgement to the art of photography which has enabled this book to come into being, and to the devoted care of its author Micheline Steinberg.

# PROLOGUE

England's theatrical centre of the nineteenth century, as today, was London. Stratford-upon-Avon was a little-known market town, with no main line railway connections. So when the prospect was mooted of a permanent building at Shakespeare's birthplace, to be erected not as a simple memorial to Shakespeare but as a working theatre, it attracted considerable ridicule:

*'And why, if there is to be a Memorial Theatre at all, should it not be in London, where Shakespeare's plays were originally produced and where many of them were written?...But why a memorial to Shakespeare at all? Are not his works his best memorial?'* (The Daily Mail). And The Observer agreed:

*'London is the only place where a company to perform the plays could be got together, or where great audiences could be collected.'*

**1.** One man, however, was not deterred by these criticisms — **Charles Edward Flower.** A member of Stratford's local brewery family, he was the Memorial Theatre's original visionary and eventual founder. By virtue of his enthusiasm and generosity, he inevitably and affectionately, acquired the nickname of, *'The Self-Raising

*Flower'*. Charles Flower's drive was spurred not merely by a desire to make his mark on posterity, but by a determined ambition to improve the art of the theatre. He intended that *'a small theatre should be established in which actors can study quietly and be instructed in the art, not the mere business, of their profession.'*

With considerable prescience he anticipated the need for today's arts complex , seeking the establishment of not only a theatre, but a drama school, a library and a picture gallery. In fact a gallery was built, and still exists today, having survived the great fire of 1926.

**2.** The Shakespeare Memorial Theatre was designed by Messrs Dodgshun and Unsworth of Westminster, London. It was not universally admired. George Bernard Shaw described it as *'An admirable building, adapted for every conceivable purpose other than that of a theatre.'* The critic, W A Darlington, agreed: *'...it looked like an ogre's castle escaped from some German fairy-tale.'* Oscar Wilde, however, considered it *'a beautiful building, one of the loveliest erected in England for many years.'*

Drawing of the SMT, c.1876.

**3.** Theatre and ornamental pond, 1885.

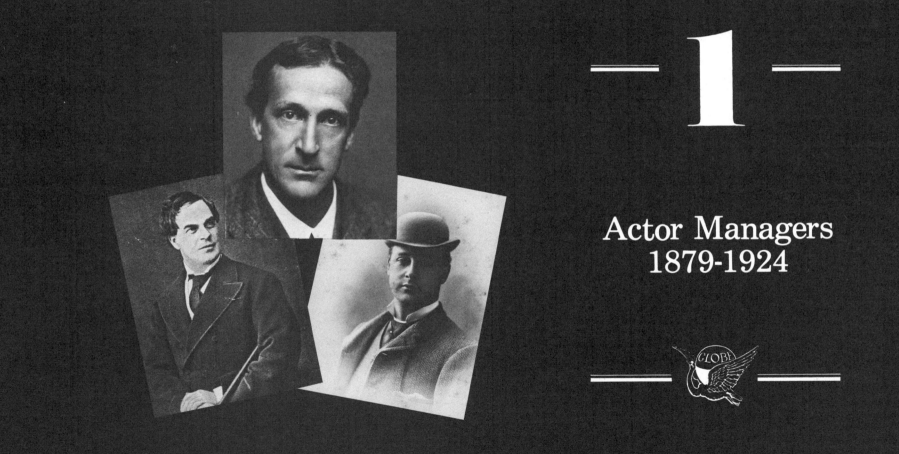

# 1

## Actor Managers
## 1879-1924

# THE OPENING OF THE SHAKESPEARE MEMORIAL THEATRE

**1. Inaugural poster** for the opening of the Shakespeare Memorial Theatre — disclosing an exhausting repertoire of plays to be produced within a week. Eight consecutive plays, beginning on 23 April, celebrated Shakespeare's birthday, hence the name 'Birthday Play'. These weeks eventually became known as Festivals. Today, most plays rehearse for six to eight weeks and the Stratford season, as it is now known, runs from mid-March to the end of January, a total of 46 weeks.

The inaugural tickets and programme were printed by Stratford's Herald Printing and Stationery Company. Nowadays, the firm still contracts for much of the RSC's work, including this publication.

**2.** In the first six years the theatre's Festivals were managed by a succession of actor-managers; the more notable amongst them included **Barry Sullivan** (1879-1880) *left,* and **Edward Compton** (1881-1882) *right.*
*Photo: Mc Lanachan*

During that opening week Sullivan cast himself as Hamlet, his 3061st performance of the role.

**3.** There are no known photographs of the Memorial Theatre's original production, **Much Ado About Nothing,** directed by its first actor-manager, Barry Sullivan. This engraving of the opening performance illustrates the narrow proscenium, then lit by gas footlights, the intimacy of the theatre, and the seemingly uncomfortable bentwood chairs.

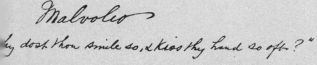

*Malvolio*

*hy dost thou smile so, & kiss thy hand so oft?"*

4

5

**4.** The Forest of Arden scene in Barry Sullivan's production of **As You Like It (1879),** in which *'the deer killing incident . . . in the fourth act . . . was made to occupy the whole stage . . . The dead deer was no mere "property" animal, but had been shot for this presentation in Charlecote Park.'* The appearance of this stuffed stag became a regular feature of productions until Nigel Playfair's in 1919.

*Photo: C.W. Smartt*

**5. Edward Compton** (father of Fay Compton and Compton Mackenzie, the author) became the Festival's second actor-manager (1881 and 1882).

He brought with him his well-known touring company, **The Compton Comedy Company,** which in following years frequently visited Stratford outside the Festival periods. His playing of the part of Jack Rover in O'Keeffe's comedy **Wild Oats,** became famous and *'would alone entitle him to a high place among English Comedians'.* (See title page). It was first performed on 27 April 1882; in 1976 at the Aldwych Theatre Alan Howard (who is related to Compton) assumed the role in the first production this century.

**6. Edward Compton** as Malvolio in **Twelfth Night** (1881) *'outdid himself . . . Every motion was expressive and pregnant with meaning. The change in demeanour from the simple steward to the pompous, bombastic, conceited and believed-to-be-accepted lover of Countess Olivia, was a splendid piece of acting.'*

11

# STRATFORD'S LEADING LADIES 1879-1902

Many well-known actresses were specially invited to the Stratford Festivals for particular performances. This practice marked the beginning of the star system which was much favoured by the actor-managers of the time, some even marrying the leading ladies then playing opposite them for the duration of the Festivals. A stage-hand at the time was heard to remark *'Call this a Shakespeare Company, it's nothin' but a bloomin' Matrimonial Agency'.*

**1. Helen Faucit** was persuaded, at the age of 68, to come out of retirement to play the leading lady to Barry Sullivan in the first performance at the Shakespeare Memorial Theatre.

**2. Miss Alleyn,** leading lady to Charles Bernard, (Director of the 1884 and 1885 Festivals). She later married him in Stratford. Of her Juliet, *'So realistic was the impersonation that the audience almost forebore to applaud the conclusion of the scene in the intensity of feeling that was caused.'*

**3. Henry VI Part 1** had its first production at the Shakespeare Memorial Theatre in 1889 under Osmond Tearle's direction. Joan La Pucelle *'was charmingly taken by* **Miss Kingsley,** *though such is the demoralising effect of the modern drama, her dress and appearance irresistibly suggested at times the Prince Charming of modern burlesque rather than the high-minded religieuse . . .'*

*Photos 2 & 3: Downey*

MEMORIAL THEATRE,
STRATFORD-ON-AVON.

THE ANNUAL SERIES OF
Dramatic Performances
For 1889, will Commence on
MONDAY, APRIL 22nd,
UNDER THE DIRECTION OF
MR. OSMOND TEARLE,
WITH A SPECIALLY ENGAGED COMPANY.

SHAKESPEARE'S BIRTHDAY, TUESDAY,
23rd, will be performed for the First Time
since his days

Shakespeare's Historical Play,
HENRY VIth, Part 1.
the direction of John O'Connor, R.I.

## MEMORIAL THEATRE,
### STRATFORD-ON-AVON

Mr ARTHUR LEWIS has the honour to announce

### MADAME

# SARAH ⁂ BERNHARDT

AS

# ✦ HAMLET. ✦

7

**"The Divine Sarah"**
**Her views on Hamlet.**
Because the original impersonator of Hamlet was a fat man, therefore the tradition has remained that the noble Dane was of stout proportions. Here again, according to my lights, is an absolute error. He was slender and supple of limb, a man of nerves and intellect, dramatic and passionate in temperament. **Daily Chronicle June 17, 1899.**

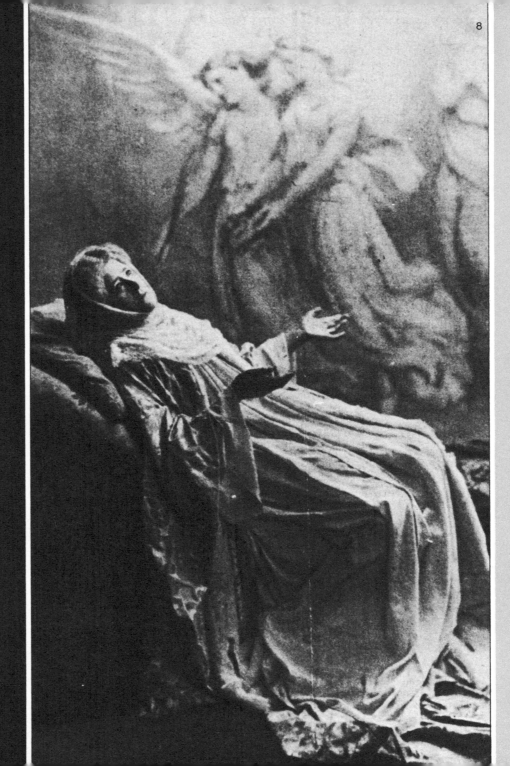

**4. Mary Anderson** was invited from the United States to give just one performance of Rosalind in **As You Like It** (1885) to raise funds for the Memorial Theatre. According to the Birmingham Daily Post *'abnormal excitment at once reigned in the theatrical world. . . There are, however, one or two points . . . which require reconsideration. . . Her habit of draping her graceful figure with a long silken cloak, which she causes her Ganymede to wear, should certainly be checked . . . it . . . invests the character with an unnecessary suggestion of prudery.'*

**5. Lillian Braithwaite** was also a 'visiting star'.

**6. Constance Featherstonhaugh** joined Frank Benson's company in 1885, married him in 1886, and continued to play leading roles with him for many years. Here, as Titania in **A Midsummer Night's Dream (c. 1886)** *'all gauze and huge butterfly wings . . . I must have spent months of life on the bank.'*

**7.** Shakespearean tradition was for boys and men to play women's roles. It was not until 1899 that **Sarah Bernhardt** turned the tables with her impersonation of **Hamlet**.

*Photo: Daniels*

**8. Ellen Terry** as Queen Katherine in the vision scene of **Henry VIII (1902).**

In an interview for The Sketch she tells how she was once cast as *'the top angel'* in Mr Charles Kean's 1855 London production of **Henry VIII:** *'There is an impression that I have steadily risen as an actress. . . As a matter of fact, after that experience I came down in the world and am now a mere Queen instead of a "top angel".'*

1. Starring invitations were not limited to actresses. **Beerbohm Tree** performed **Hamlet (1910)** at the Memorial Theatre. *'Is this kind thought for me?'*, he asked, when he arrived to find the streets decorated with flags for Shakespeare's birthday.

*Photo: Downey, from the Theatre Royal Haymarket, 1892.*

2. **Forbes-Robertson** as **Hamlet,** which he played at the Memorial Theatre in 1908.

*Photo: From the Lyceum Theatre, 1897.*

1. **Frank Benson** was the leading actor-manager of his generation. His energy and drive transformed the Shakespeare Memorial Theatre from a seven-day Festival into an internationally renowned theatre company. During his reign (1886-1919) he directed all but five of the Stratford Festivals, which grew from one week a year in 1886 to a Spring Festival of two to three weeks a year, to which was added a four-week Summer Festival by 1914. With the support of the theatre's founder, Charles Edward Flower, Frank Benson spread the fame of the company by touring it nationally and abroad. Many actors remained with the company throughout Benson's years and later, became known as the 'Bensonians'. Members of that company can now be seen depicted on the stained-glass windows of the theatre's gallery, known as the Bensonian Room. By 1919 *'there were more than a hundred actors playing principal parts in London theatres who had taken part in the Stratford Festivals.'*

2. **Benson** as **Henry V (1898),** playing opposite his wife, **Constance's** Katharine of France.

*The Merry Wives of Windsor, The Taming of the Shrew* and *The Merchant of Venice* were the three plays most frequently performed by the Benson company; so much so that the repertoire became popularly known as *'The Merry Shrews of Venice'*.

**1. Benson** as Caliban in **The Tempest (c.1897),** *'always insisted on appearing with a real fish in his mouth. Sometimes the property man would forget to renew this piece of realism . . . which was most distressing to Benson and indeed to everyone on the stage.'*

**2.** As Romeo in **Romeo and Juliet (c. 1887).**

*Photo: Bassano.*

**3.** During a performance of **The Merchant of Venice (c.1896).** Having heard of his daughter's birth, Frank Benson added to Shylock's lines *'I have a daughter but only a little one!'*

*Photo: Bassano.*

Lizzie
Caswell Smith

**4.** As **Henry V (1897)** the Birthday Play of that year and the play's first production at the SMT, played without the Chorus. The part was one of Benson's favourites; he played it several times until 1912 when he was over 50.

*Photo: Chancellor*

**5.** As **Macbeth (c.1905-1906)** which he was still playing in 1931. He wears the vast feather that Richmond (Benson's personal Valet) — who had the weekly task of packing it — insisted *'had fallen from a wing of the Archangel Gabriel'.*

*Photo: Beagles*

**6. Benson** played the title role in the first Stratford production of **Timon of Athens (1892).**

*Photo: Chancellor*

*Over page*
**7. Benson** as **Richard II (1897).** The critic C.E. Montague wrote in 1899: *'Mr Benson brings out admirably that half of the character which criticism seems always to have taken pains to obscure — the capable and faithful artist in the same skin as the incapable and unfaithful king'.*

*Photo: Kilpatrick, Belfast*

**8.** The setting for the lists scene from **Richard II (1896).** The Bensonian motto was: *'We few, we happy few, we band of brothers,'* and his company was widely regarded as *'the nursery of modern Shakespearean acting'.* Many Bensonians continued with the company into the 1930s and Frank Benson became known as 'Pa' to generations of actors.

MEMORIAL THEATRE
STRATFORD·ON·AVON
Mʳ·F·R·BENSON'S COMPANY

APRIL·14·TO·MAY·3·1902

Benson's methods were not always orthodox: he inspired actors with his athletic zeal quite as much as with his artistic ideals, and no young actor was allowed to escape the discipline of hockey, added to the training of the histrionic art.

Benson selected his actors for their sporting proficiency as well as their acting ability. He wired one player *'Can you play Rugby tomorrow?'*. The actor agreed, turning up for rehearsal the following morning without knowing a word of the part. He had no inkling, he explained, that *'Rugby'* referred to the part in *'Merry Wives'*. . .

Some of these Bensonians included:

**1. Oscar Asche** as Thomas Mowbray, Duke of Norfolk in **Richard II (1896)** — a staunch old Bensonian.

**2. Frank Rodney** as Bolingbroke also in Benson's production of **Richard II (1896)** of whom James Agate wrote in 1929 *'The best*. . . *Bolingbroke*. . . *I have seen'*.

**1. George Weir** in **The Merry Wives of Windsor** (1902)
'*loathed his mechanical stomach . . . Hence Falstaff's alarm one night when his false stomach gradually collapsed during the play and had to be inflated at any convenient interval*'.
**George Fitzgerald** (Page), **George Weir** (Falstaff), **Frank Rodney** (Ford), **Constance Benson** (Mrs Ford), **Frances Dillon** (Mrs Page).

**2. Benson** as Hamlet (1902). Behind him, **Harcourt Williams** as Horatio.

**3. Benson** as Petruchio in **The Taming of The Shrew** (1910) taking **Constance Benson** (Katharina) off to Padua on a donkey — '*business that would cause infinite worry and a great many bruises when Constance Benson had to have a fresh untrained donkey week by week when they went on the provincial circuit*'.

**4.** The Bensonian repertoire did not confine itself to Shakespeare: **Don Quixote** (1907) with **Benson** in the title part and **George Weir** as Sancho Panza.

Benson was an early supporter of the revival of Greek Tragedy in British theatre, having acted in and produced **The Orestean Trilogy** of Aeschylus while at Oxford. He reproduced this production in Stratford with the same set, originally designed by William Richmond and Alma Tadema. The production included '*a trained female chorus*,' but was not popular. The plays were not repeated by the RSC until John Barton's production of **The Greeks** (1980).

**5. The Libation Bearers** (c.1904) **Constance Benson**, (Clytemnestra); **Frank Benson** (Orestes).

20

**Sir F. R. Benson Famous Actor Knighted**
While the King was congratulating the actor, the management of the theatre, acting upon a suggestion conveyed to them, were busily engaged looking for a sword with which an accolade could be bestowed. A member of the staff was able to procure one promptly, and Mr Benson was duly knighted.
**Daily Telegraph May 3, 1916.**

7

8

9

10

11

12

**6. Baliol Holloway** as **Richard III (c. 1923)** — one of his favourite parts. He first joined the Bensonians in 1911 and remained under Bridges-Adams as actor/director. When offered the choice of a part in Romeo and Juliet *'Well, I'm not quite sure what part to play — 'Mercutio' and get off early, or the 'Friar' and keep my trousers on!'*

**7.** Part of the 'Bensonian tradition' was 'singing' Shakespeare, in contrast to the present-day more naturalistic approach. **Henry Ainley** as Romeo in **Romeo and Juliet (c.1908)** was one of the foremost lyrical actors of the Benson company.

**8. Matheson Lang** as **Hamlet (1909),** whom he played as a 'Romantic'.
*Photo: Foulsham & Banfield*

Because of the difficulties of photographic technique, many of the photographs of the period were taken outside the theatre.

**9. Lewis Waller** as **Henry V (1911).**

**10. Dorothy Green** as Cleopatra, and

**11. Randle Ayrton** as Enobarbus in **Antony and Cleopatra (1912).**

**12. Murray Carrington** as **Macbeth (1920).**

In due course, Benson received Royal recognition for his work and was knighted on stage in the Drury Lane Theatre London. (See newspaper quote)

Some of the famous-to-be started their careers on the stage of the old Memorial Theatre.

**1. Edith** (later Dame Edith) **Evans,** first stage part was an Elizabethan Cressida in William Poel's Elizabethan Stage Society production of **Troilus and Cressida (1912).** Also appearing in that production:

**2. Hermione Gingold** attired in Greek costume as Cassandra. The production was also notable for the casting of women in men's roles; it was Poel's opinion that if he cast a man as Thersites *'he would be sure to over-act'.*

**3. Laurence Olivier** made his debut on the Stratford stage with the All Saints Church Choir School, London, in their all male production of **The Taming of the Shrew (1922)** but even then a perceptive critic noticed that this *'Katharina has fire of her own . . . You feel that if an apple were thrown to this Katharina she would instinctively try to catch it in her lap and . . . we hope . . . that someone will make the experiment.'* As for Olivier, he later said *'That, of course, was an amateur appearance, but my first sniff of a real theatre from 'that' side of the footlights'.*

Olivier as Katharina before and after make-up.

**4.** As Katharina again, with Petruchio.

# Troilus and Cressida

## Characters in the Play

**THE TROJANS.**
PRIAM
HECTOR
TROILUS       } his sons
PARIS
HELENUS
AENEAS        } generals
ANTENOR
CALCHAS, with the Greeks
PANDARUS
MARGARELON
ANDROMACHE, Hector's wife
CASSANDRA, Priam's daughter
CRESSIDA, Calchas' daughter

**THE GREEKS.**
AGAMEMNON
MENELAUS, his brother
ACHILLES
AJAX
ULYSSES       } generals
NESTOR
DIOMEDES
PATROCLUS
THERSITES
ALEXANDER
HELEN, with the Trojans

## Names of the Actors in the order in which they appear

*Prologue*, WILLIAM SINGER ; *Troilus*, ION SWINLEY ; *Pandarus*, WILLIAM POEL ; *Troilus' boy*, GRACE WALFORD ; *Aeneas*, MADGE WHITEMAN ; *Alexander*, GRACE LAURENCE ; *Cressida*, EDITH EVANS ; *Agamemnon*, ANTHONY WARDE ; *Nestor*, H. B. BARWELL ; *Ulysses*, KENYON MUSGRAVE ; *Menelaus*, ARCHIBALD McLEAN ; *Diomedes*, HERBERT RANSON ; *Ajax*, ROLLO BALMAIN ; *Thersites*, ELSPETH KEITH ; *Achilles*, WILLIAM H. BAKER ; *Patroclus*, ROBERT CAREY ; *Priam*, EWART WHEELER ; *Hector*, P. L. EYRE ; *Paris*, MAY CAREY ; *Helenus*, GABRIELLE HARRIS ; *Cassandra*, HERMIONE GINGOLD ; *Helen*, ENID LORIMER ; *Calchas*, WILLIAM SINGER ; *Andromache*, MURIEL DOLE.

*Assistant Stage Managers*—HERBERT RANSON and JAMES C. TAYLOR.

During the First World War, the theatre made its contribution to the war effort, making facilities available to light entertainers such as **Jack Buchanan.**

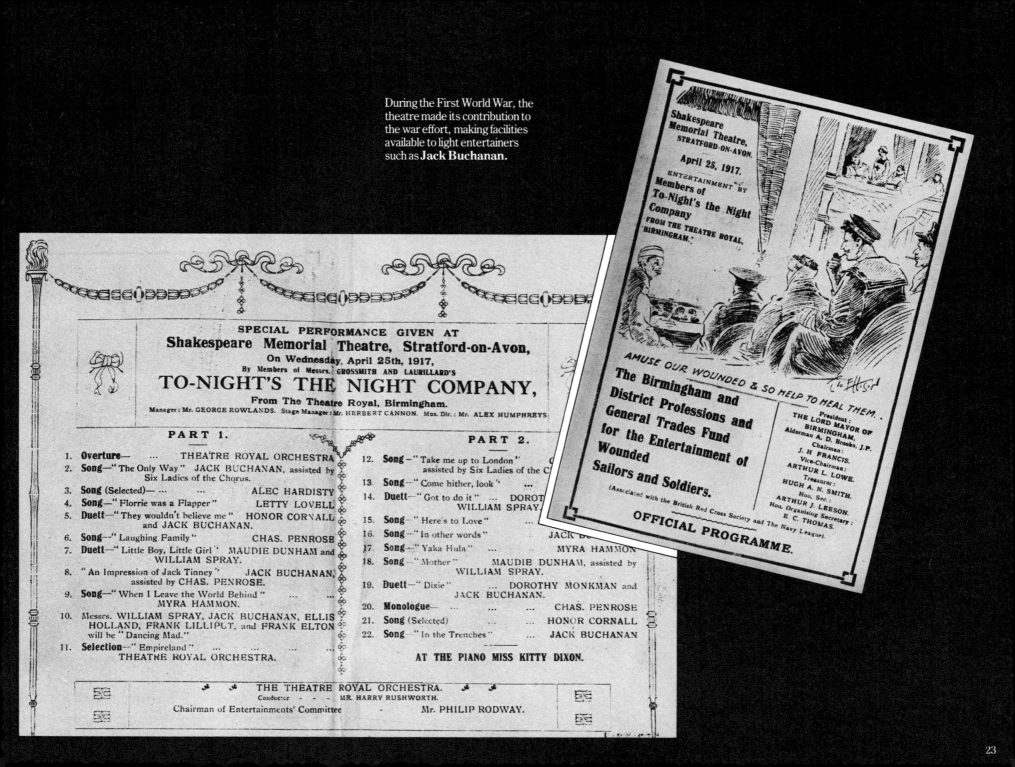

SPECIAL PERFORMANCE GIVEN AT

## Shakespeare Memorial Theatre, Stratford-on-Avon,

On Wednesday, April 25th, 1917,

By Members of Messrs. GROSSMITH AND LAURILLARD'S

# TO-NIGHT'S THE NIGHT COMPANY,

From The Theatre Royal, Birmingham.

Manager : Mr. GEORGE ROWLANDS.   Stage Manager : Mr. HERBERT CANNON.   Mus. Dir. : Mr. ALEX HUMPHREYS

### PART 1.

1. **Overture**— ...   THEATRE ROYAL ORCHESTRA
2. **Song**—"The Only Way"  JACK BUCHANAN, assisted by Six Ladies of the Chorus.
3. **Song** (Selected)— ...   ALEC HARDISTY
4. **Song**—"Florrie was a Flapper"   LETTY LOVELL
5. **Duett**—"They wouldn't believe me"  HONOR CORNALL and JACK BUCHANAN.
6. **Song**—"Laughing Family"   CHAS. PENROSE
7. **Duett**—"Little Boy, Little Girl"  MAUDIE DUNHAM and WILLIAM SPRAY.
8. "An Impression of Jack Tinney"   JACK BUCHANAN, assisted by CHAS. PENROSE.
9. **Song**—"When I Leave the World Behind" ...   MYRA HAMMON.
10. Messrs. WILLIAM SPRAY, JACK BUCHANAN, ELLIS HOLLAND, FRANK LILLIPUT, and FRANK ELTON will be "Dancing Mad."
11. **Selection**—"Empireland" ... ... THEATRE ROYAL ORCHESTRA.

### PART 2.

12. **Song**—"Take me up to London" ... assisted by Six Ladies of the C[horus]
13. **Song**—"Come hither, look" ...
14. **Duett**—"Got to do it" ...  DOROT[HY] WILLIAM SPRAY.
15. **Song**—"Here's to Love" ...
16. **Song**—"In other words" ...   JACK B[UCHANAN]
17. **Song**—"Yaka Hula" ... ...   MYRA HAMMON
18. **Song**—"Mother"   MAUDIE DUNHAM, assisted by WILLIAM SPRAY.
19. **Duett**—"Dixie" ...  DOROTHY MONKMAN and JACK BUCHANAN.
20. **Monologue**— ... ... ...   CHAS. PENROSE
21. **Song** (Selected) ... ...   HONOR CORNALL
22. **Song** "In the Trenches" ...   JACK BUCHANAN

**AT THE PIANO MISS KITTY DIXON.**

♣  ♣  THE THEATRE ROYAL ORCHESTRA.  ♣  ♣
Conductor - - - MR. HARRY RUSHWORTH.
Chairman of Entertainments' Committee - MR. PHILIP RODWAY.

---

Shakespeare Memorial Theatre, STRATFORD-ON-AVON.

**April 25, 1917.**

ENTERTAINMENT BY Members of To-Night's the Night Company FROM THE THEATRE ROYAL, BIRMINGHAM.

AMUSE OUR WOUNDED & SO HELP TO HEAL THEM.

**The Birmingham and District Professions and General Trades Fund** for the Entertainment of Wounded Sailors and Soldiers.

(Associated with the British Red Cross Society and The Navy League).

President : THE LORD MAYOR OF BIRMINGHAM, Alderman A. D. Brooks, J.P.
Chairman : J. H. FRANCIS.
Vice-Chairman : ARTHUR L. LOWE.
Treasurer : HUGH A. N. SMITH.
Hon. Sec. : ARTHUR J. LRESON.
Hon. Organising Secretary : E. C. THOMAS.

# OFFICIAL PROGRAMME.

1. In 1919, **Nigel Playfair** was invited to produce **As You Like It,** with non-realistic stage designs by Claud Lovat Frazer. After the first performance he found himself treated as a '*national criminal*' for the disposal of the by now moth-eaten stag, whilst Lovat Frazer was told in no uncertain terms by a local member of the audience '*Young man . . . how dare you meddle with our Shakespeare!*'

**Nigel Playfair** (first Forest Lord) in **As You Like It (1919).**

2. Frank Benson's successor as first full-time director of the Festival was **W. Bridges-Adams.** He was determined '*to play Shakespeare . . . as far as possible unbowdlerised . . .*' As a result of this policy he acquired the nickname of '*Unabridges Adams*'.

3. The company was renamed **The New Shakespeare Company,** and improvements to the theatre were carried out:

'*. . . It has long been admitted that electricity is the best light for stage effects.*'

4. **Interior of the Memorial Theatre (c.1926)** shows altered proscenium arch and dress circle shape dating from c. 1903/4. This intimate Victorian horse-shoe theatre seated approximately 740 people. The Act drop, painted by W.R. Beverley, depicts a state procession of Queen Elizabeth to the Globe Theatre in Southwark.

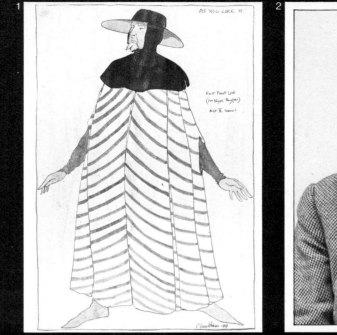

SHAKESPEARE BIRTHDAY FESTIVAL
April 23rd to May 19th, 1923

SHAKESPEARE MEMORIAL

PERFORMANCES BY
THE NEW SHAKESPEARE COMPANY
Under the Direction of W. Bridges Adams

**A NATIONAL DEBT.**

Mr. Peson (to John Bull). "GOOD MY LORD, WILL YOU SEE THE PLAYERS WELL
BESTOWED? . . . USE THEM AFTER YOUR OWN HONOUR AND DIGNITY."

*Hamlet*—Act II., Scene 2.

# 2

# Triumphs and Disasters
# 1925-1932

In 1925 the Memorial Theatre was granted its Royal Charter, whose preamble promised '*the advancement of Shakespearean drama and literature both in this Country and in Our Dominions beyond the Seas.*'

But with no possibility of a State subsidy, the theatre launched an endowment appeal – which failed to reach its target. George Bernard Shaw, a frequent visitor to the Memorial Theatre, supported the appeal and was, as ever, sharply critical – and prophetic:

'*Stratford is not complete. It wants a new theatre. The Memorial Theatre is an admirable building for any purpose except that of a theatre. In Shakespeare's day it was the trick of the dramatist to produce plays which would make people forget the discomforts of the auditorium, but now the cinema has come along and accustomed the British public to comfortable theatres. The public therefore, will not long put up with the Stratford Theatre. I will say nothing about the ventilation because one cannot discuss what does not exist. When you have to deal with the plays of Shakespeare, plays of the right length, which I myself use — three and a half hours — with only one interval, the theatre at Stratford, above all others in the world, should have comfortable seats and you know what they are! As for the stage, one cannot be satisfied with the sort of makeshifts that have to be made at present in order to play the plays of Shakespeare in one scene . . . You must get a new stage, and a new front of the house.*'
**Birmingham Mail, April 1925**

**Punch Cartoon, April 1923.**
*(See previous page).*

26

'Destruction of the Memorial Theatre Stratford-on-Avon by Fire March 6th 1926

**Better Burned!**
**G.B.S. Welcomes the news:**
**Why not Shakespeare in Tent?**
'I am extremely glad to hear it', said Mr. George Bernard Shaw when informed of the fire . . . 'Stratford-on-Avon is to be congratulated . . . It is very cheerful news.'
'It will be a tremendous advantage to have a proper modern theatre. There are a few other theatres I would like to see burned down.
'I don't expect an ideal theatre built at Stratford-on-Avon. I merely want to see a good working theatre. In the meantime, I suppose, they will have to play Shakespeare there in a tent, but I do not see why they should not'. **Sunday Herald, 7 March 1926.**

1. A year later, 6 March 1926, the theatre was, in an hour, gutted by fire, with only the outer walls remaining and the adjoining museum and art gallery saved.

2. **Bridges-Adams** (second from right, looking down into the ruined auditorium) was forced to comment on malicious gossip: '*It has been said that the burning of the theatre is a blessing in disguise. At the moment, we are preoccupied with disguise.*'

3. The fire received wide press coverage, predictably fuelled by Shaw's comments.

4. Shortly after, in fact, the Stratford Picture House was converted and served as a temporary home from 1926-1932. It was even praised by some:

'*The Shakespeare Birthday Festival opened here last night in a picture theatre — a theatre contrasting in many ways to the old Memorial. The auditorium is wide and well arranged, there is a comfortable tip-up seat for every patron, the members of the orchestra appear in full view instead of emitting their strains mysteriously from a hidden chasm. The gallery provides an original touch, for it is on the ground floor at the back of the pit.
In truth, this picture house in Greenhill Street forms an excellent substitute for the burned Memorial Theatre. One hears well from any part and the stage is of adequate dimensions.*' **Birmingham Mail, 13 April 1926.**

**1.** The sets and wardrobe having been destroyed in the fire, Bridges-Adams organised a fund-raising tour to America. Meanwhile, gifts poured in to replace some of the losses. **Fabia Drake** remembers playing one matinée performance as Viola in **Twelfth Night (1926)** at the Picture House, before setting off on tour. She wore a costume sent from America by Sam Sothern and Julia Marlowe, who had formed an acclaimed American Shakespearean company.
*Photo: Claude Harris*

**2.** All the shows in the Picture House were directed by **Bridges-Adams,** and included a number of Bensonians.

**Randle Ayrton** (Ford) and **Roy Byford** (Falstaff) in **The Merry Wives of Windsor (1931).**
*Photo: Claude Harris*

**3. Ayrton** in the title role of **Macbeth (1931)** with **Dorothy Massingham** (Lady Macbeth).
*Photo: Claude Harris*

The Cinema was demolished in 1983 to make way for a supermarket.

**4**

**Archibald Flower** had been appointed the Chairman of the Shakespeare Memorial Theatre in 1903, in succession to his father; in a letter to The Times (11 April 1926) he wrote: *'The new building must provide, not only for the present needs but to the future. . . Shakespeare calls for intimacy as well as breadth . . . to provide a much-needed Conference Hall and space to exhibit many objects of great interest in connexion with the history of the stage.'*

Following a competition for the design of a new theatre, in 1927 the Committee accepted **Elisabeth Scott's** entry.

**4.** The design of the auditorium eschewed the previous intimate horseshoe shape, and offered a direct line of view on to the stage. While it had the incidental effect of distancing actor from audience, it enlarged the theatre's capacity by one-third — to 1000 seats.

The new theatre received mixed reviews. The Daily Express called it *'The New Soviet Barracks at Stratford'*.

The Manchester Guardian was inconsistent: *'The theatre is a characteristic monument — solid and unlikely, perhaps, ever to be of much use theatrically except on ceremonial occasions'*, (23 April 1932), but also *'Stratford has now the finest working theatre in England'*, (Ivor Brown, 25 April 1932).

**5.** A romantic view of the new theatre's exterior at night.
*Photo: Jerome Ltd*

The safety curtain, painted by Vladimir Polounin, was in use between 1932 and 1959. *(See over page).*

Stratford·upon·Avon

SAFETY CURTAIN

# 3

## A New Theatre:
## A New Look
## 1932-1945

The next decade saw a revolution in production styles and set designs, led by key figures such as W Bridges-Adams, Theodore Komisarjevsky, Norman Wilkinson, Aubrey Hammond, and Motley. Added to this creative upsurge was the introduction of acting talent, much otherwise untried, including Fabia Drake, Rachel Kempson, Trevor Howard, John Laurie, Alec Clunes and Clement McCallin. Leading roles were taken by Randle Ayrton, Baliol Holloway and Donald Wolfit. It was an exciting and controversial decade during which the established and traditional approaches were challenged.

In 1932, at Bridges-Adams' request, **Sir Frank Benson** (then in his seventies) was asked to perform Shylock at a special matinée of **The Merchant of Venice** with an entire cast of old Bensonians as an homage to the new generation of players; Bridges-Adams' wife exclaimed, '*now I feel that the theatre has been blessed*'.

**1.** The Prince of Wales attended the opening production, **Henry IV Parts 1 and 2,** led by **Randle Ayrton.** The same plays were to open the RSC's new Barbican Theatre in 1982, with Patrick Stewart in the title role.

**2.** Another innovation in the 1932 opening production was the casting of a young (28) actor as Hal, **Gyles Isham.** (In 1984, an even younger actor played an older Hal when 23-year-old Kenneth Branagh took the lead in **Henry V.**)

*Photos: Claude Harris*

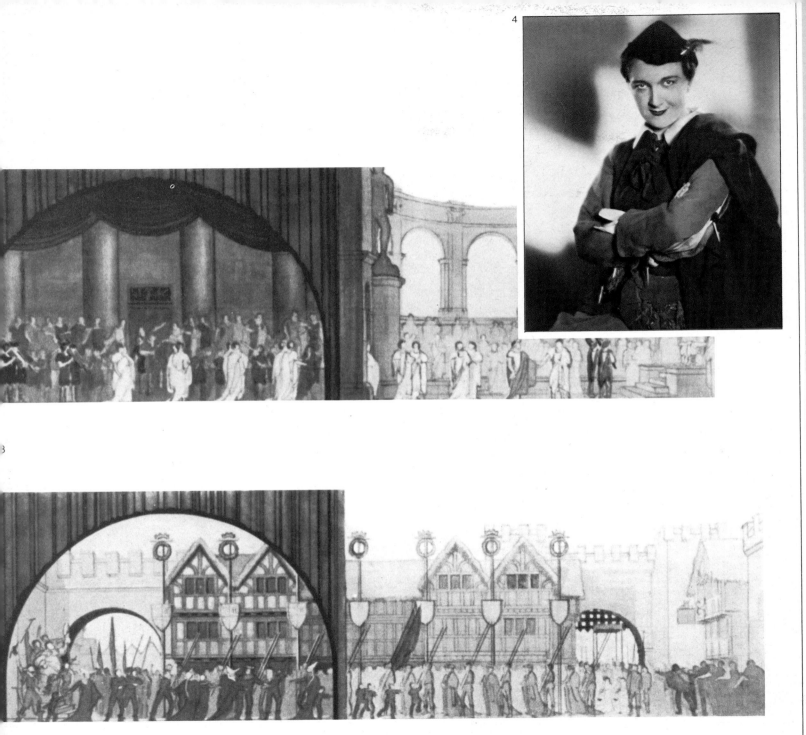

3. According to Fabia Drake, *'1932 opened badly because it was inaudible'*, due to the wide bays on either side of the stage, designed to take the rolling stages. If an actor turned sideways, his voice disappeared into the wings. But others welcomed the new technology: *'Mr Bridges-Adams had made spectacular use of his rolling stage by showing Caesar passing in procession along the street to the Senate House, while the scenery moved against the direction of the march. What a wonder this would have seemed in the old Stratford — and what a wonder, indeed it is!'* **Daily Telegraph, 5 May 1932.**

Production sketches for **Julius Caesar (1932)** top and **Henry IV part 2 (1932).**

4. **Fabia Drake** was the first actress to play major roles in the new theatre. In her portrayal of Rosalind in **As You Like It (1932)** she felt that the Elizabethan short cropped wig was an attempt to make more of Rosalind's male role: *'I wanted to look like a boy'*, and she succeeded: *'Miss Fabia Drake gave us the best individual performance we have yet had during the present Festival. Her Rosalind did not lack tenderness and courtly refinement, nor did it miss the humour'.* **The Times, 28 November 1932.**

# THEODORE KOMISARJEVSKY

**1. Theodore Komisarjevsky** was to become '*the theatre's chartered revolutionary*'. His production of **The Merchant of Venice (1932)** was a turning point for the Stratford theatre. Not everyone appreciated his comedy version which was described as '*a bomb for Stratford*' and as '*the histrionic Venice of the untravelled Elizabethan*'. The controversial notices drew large audiences to Stratford.

**2. Randle Ayrton** as Shylock, described by Wolfit as '*the finest study of the part I ever saw*'. Photograph taken from a later production of **The Merchant of Venice (1935).**
*Photo: Anthony*

**3. Fabia Drake** (Portia) considered Komisarjevsky '*gave a springboard for comedy*'. **The Merchant of Venice (1932).**
*Photo: Anthony*

**4. John Dennis** (Launcelot Gobbo) **The Merchant of Venice (1932).**
*Photo: Anthony*

**5.** Komisarjevsky's design for the opening scenes of **The Merchant of Venice (1932).**

34

## A weird production

'Komisarjevsky tonight had the honour of being the first guest producer to stage a play in the new Shakespeare Memorial Theatre . . . he has fantastic-alised *The Merchant of Venice* beyond all knowledge . . .'
**W. A. Darlington, Daily Telegraph, 26 July 1932.**

## Crazy Night at Stratford

'He produced the play against a background of fantastic Venetian scenery of his own design. The pillar of St Mark's leaned drunkenly against a nightmare Venetian tower surrounded by a confusion of flying bridges. The set was riotously out of perspective and bathed in a pink glow. . . He began and ended the play with a dance of grotesque figures to music by Bach, and dressed his actors . . . with an extravagance of plumes, ruffs and cloaks'.
**Daily Express, 26 July 1932.**

1. In 1933, Komisarjevsky followed up with a similarly controversial **Macbeth,** criticised as *'futurist'* in the same derogatory fashion as had been Playfair's *As You Like It* of 1919.

The set was entirely in aluminium and relied heavily on lighting effects — Banquo's ghost was conjured up by Macbeth's reflection. The Times damned it as *'Producer's Shakespeare'.*

2. **Fabia Drake** (Lady Macbeth) found it difficult to work on such a set; Komisarjevsky had asked them *'to rub oil on their skin so that they would shine against the metallic set and the steepness in the sleepwalking scene was nerve-racking'.*

3. Lady Macbeth's crown, made of scouring pads, provoked a member of the audience to write: *'I have much pleasure in sending, with compliments, a couple of extra bosses for Lady Macbeth's head and neck dress, and a new pair of epaulettes each for Macbeth and Macduff, as I noticed last night (Thursday) that some spares might be useful.*

*Joking apart, I think it shameful that your time and energies should be wasted in such an atrocious production as this one of Shakespeare's Macbeth, and that you should be dressed up in costumes trimmed with kitchen utensils from a penny bazaar. . . . I marvel how you all did so well in such ludicrous surroundings.'*

4. **George Hayes** (Macbeth).
*Photos: Anthony*

**1.** The climax of the decade was the combination of **Komisarjevsky** (director/designer), **Randle Ayrton** and **Donald Wolfit** in **King Lear (1936).**

Komisarjevsky explained: *'I am producing it for the sake of the acting, and not for the mise-en-scène. I have no sets (except the simplest) and no décors. I am not giving it a "barbaric" atmosphere or surroundings or costumes, because to my mind there is nothing barbaric about the play. It is inspired by the ideas of the Renaissance period. . .'.* Despite the minimalist design, there were technical difficulties: actors found the steps too narrow and had to negotiate them in a *'crab-like fashion'*. However, Ayrton's Lear was one of the greatest of the century.

Opening scene — *'the tulip-shaped trumpets were very impressive and the permanent cyclorama of clouds suggested a threatening storm'*.

*Photo: Daniels*

**2.** The production was revived in 1937, with **Godfrey Kenton** (Edgar), **Andrew Leigh** (Fool) and **Donald Wolfit** (Kent).

*Photo: Daniels*

**3.** A few years later, Komisarjevsky's production of **The Comedy of Errors (1938)** was said to *'blush at no experiment'*.

*Photo: Daniels*

**4. James Dale** (Antipholus of Syracuse) and **Andrew Leigh** (Dromio of Ephesus) **The Comedy of Errors (1938).**

*Photo: Daniels*

4

3

1. **Rachel Kempson,** having just left RADA at 21, joined the Memorial Theatre to play Juliet, in a production of **Romeo and Juliet (1933),** directed by **Bridges-Adams,** with **John Wyse** (Romeo).

*Photo: Anthony*

*'Miss Rachel Kempson, who has youth and grace, brings to Juliet a pale, cool, beauty which seems at first too faint in hue for its purpose but, as the need grows, puts on a glorious intensity of its own. Her delivery of the lines might be more musical, but it is unaffected, and besides giving freshness and spontaneity to familiar passages it has the emotional power which belongs to sincerity. Whether ecstatic on the wings of happiness or distractedly rushing on death, her feeling is deep and true, and only escapes her control on rare and almost always lesser occasions.'* **The Times, 21 June 1933.**

2. The following year, **Bridges-Adams** directed his final production at the Memorial Theatre: **Love's Labour's Lost (1934)** with **Rachel Kempson** (The Princess of France).

*Photo: Daniels*

3. Productions benefited from diverse designers' influence. **Aubrey Hammond's** designs for Bridges-Adams' **Love's Labour's Lost (1934)** adopt a classical realism, reminiscent of Gainsborough.

4. In contrast, **Norman Wilkinson** demonstrates his use of operatic sense in the Masque scene of Bridges-Adams' production of **The Tempest (1934)** which included costumes by Rex Whistler.

*Photo: Daniels*

**Ben Iden Payne** (1934-1942), described as a 'scholar director', replaced Bridges-Adams as Festival Director.

He directed the Coronation production of **Henry V (1937),** designed by Herbert Norris and Aubrey Hammond.

5. **Clement McCallin** as **Henry V** in the breach scene at Harfleur.

*Photo: Daniels*

# DONALD WOLFIT

**1.** Ben Iden Payne invited **Donald Wolfit** to join the company in 1936. Wolfit was 34 and played numerous roles in Iden Payne's productions over two seasons before becoming an actor-manager in his own touring company.

In **Hamlet (1937),** which the critic, James Agate, described as '*a bourgeois Hamlet*'.

*Photo: Anthony*

**2.** As Touchstone in **As You Like It (1937)** with *(left)* **Joyce Bland** (Rosalind) and *(far right)* **Valerie Tudor** (Celia). Designs by Barbara Heseltine.

**3.** As Autolycus in **The Winter's Tale (1937).**

*Photo: Daniels*

**4.** As Iachimo in **Cymbeline (1937)** with **Godfrey Kenton** (Posthumus), **Gerald Kay Souper** (Philario), and *(far right)* **George Hagar** (a Frenchman). Designs by John Gower Parks.

*Photo: Anthony*

1. The set for **A Midsummer Night's Dream (1937),** is the same one as used in the play's production originally designed by Norman Wilkinson for the opening season of the new theatre in 1932. It continued to be used until 1944.

For the Bensonian, **Randle Ayrton,** *(far left)* the role of Quince was to be one of his last before retirement. **Richard Blatchley** (Flute), **Denis Roberts** (Snout), **Baliol Holloway** (Bottom), and **Gerald Kay Souper** (Starveling).

*Photo: Daniel*

2. Iden Payne's production of **Henry VIII (1938)** included **Phyllis Neilson-Terry,** John Gielgud's cousin, (Queen Katherine), *(front left)* **Gerald Kay Souper** (Campeius), **Gyles Isham** (Henry VIII) **James Dale** (Wolsey) and *(far right)* **Kenneth Wickstead** (Griffith). Set designs by Herbert Norris.

**1.** The set by Herbert Norris for **Richard III (1939)**, was a return to the neo-Gothic style which John Laurie found '*old-fashioned*'.
*(left to right)* **Trevor Howard** (Hastings), **John Laurie** (Richard), **James Dale** (Buckingham) and **Stanley Howlett** (Stanley).

*Photos: Daniels*

**2. Irene Hentschl** was the first full-time woman director at Stratford. She brought with her three women designers collectively known as 'Motley'. In contrast to the Gothic trend, Hentschl and Motley set their production of **Twelfth Night (1939)** in the early Victorian period, and the staging was kept comparatively stark.
**John Laurie** (Malvolio) with **Leslie Brook** (Olivia, *centre*) and her household in '*heavy mourning*'.

After 1939, the Midlands began to suffer from the effects of the bombing. **Jack Watling,** who joined the company that year under the direction of the Bensonian, Baliol Holloway, suggests that '*the Germans used the roof of the Memorial Theatre as a marker — they flew along the Avon and turned right at the Theatre (the roof being white) and on to Coventry*'. During the War, the lack of funds and the difficulty of maintaining a full company, largely because of enlistment (young players were likely to be called up at any time during the season) threatened production standards; actors also accepted a reduction in earnings. But the theatre was dark for only a month during the War. Surprisingly, audience numbers were sustained, many being evacuees from nearby towns.

A sporting anecdote in the Bensonian tradition is told by the actor **John McCallum:**
*'On a fine, sunny afternoon, September 1st 1939, I was on the eighteenth green of the Stratford-on-Avon Golf Club. We were putting to see who would win the match when Michael Gwynn reached the green and said — "The Germans have invaded Poland". We all stood still for a second or two. Then Geoffrey Keen, without saying a word, and in the best Francis Drake tradition, finished his putt, sank it, and won the match.'*

**1.** Some of the productions of that time included old Bensonians.

**Coriolanus (1939),** directed by **Iden Payne. Alec Clunes** (Coriolanus) and **Dorothy Green,** the Bensonian, (Volumnia).

**2. Othello (1939),** directed by **Robert Atkins. John Laurie** (Othello) and **Alec Clunes** (Iago).

*Photos: Daniels*

3. **The Merchant of Venice (1940),** directed by **Iden Payne**. **Baliol Holloway** (Shylock *centre*) and **Thea Holme** (Portia).

*Photo: Daniels*

4. In 1942, Ben Iden Payne resigned; in 1944, **Robert Atkins** was invited to direct for two seasons. As Sir Toby Belch, in his own production of **Twelfth Night (1945).**

5. In 1945, Atkins invited the American star, **Claire Luce,** to play the leading role for that season. She attracted considerable publicity; **Graham Crowden,** who was taken on by Robert Atkins as a walk-on, remembers: *'She was glamorous, delightful and extremely gifted. She trailed clouds of heady and exotic perfumes in her wake, on stage and in the wings — perfumes which were either unobtainable or exhorbitant in price in war-time Britain'.*

*See over*

45

**Claire Luce** as Cleopatra in her
1945 season as leading lady to
Robert Atkins.

# 4

## 'Productions
## before Profits'
## 1945-1948

In 1946, **Sir Barry Jackson,** the founder and director of the Birmingham Repertory Theatre, was appointed Director of the theatre, to lead the Memorial Theatre into its post-war development. In his inaugural speech, Jackson proclaimed what were to be the two key elements of his reign: first that, *'quality in acting and production should take place over profits';* and secondly, that the director was the keyman of the theatre so that, *'at least if one man produces a play, his mistakes are consistent'*.

He duly proceeded to engage different 'producers' (directors) for each play, (who in turn engaged designers of their choice) including the young Peter Brook, who had worked with him in Birmingham, and Michael Benthall, who brought with him the actor Robert Helpmann.

During this post-war renaissance at the SMT, Jackson was careful to nurture young actors of promise, such as Paul Scofield and Donald Sinden, giving them the opportunity to work alongside more established players like Robert Harris and Valerie Taylor. Rehearsal periods were extended by scheduling eight plays to open over a period of months. The new format did not please many of the Stratford locals, who had come to expect a diet of six plays a week. Peter Brook, however, later considered that Barry Jackson had *'changed the theatre's destiny . . . after him, it became, I suppose, a success story'*.

**1. Sir Barry Jackson** in the library of the Memorial Theatre, examining the First Folio edition of Shakespeare's plays.

48

**2. Walter Hudd** directed the non-Shakespearian play, **Dr Faustus (1946),** with designs by Riette Sturge-Moore.

The Seven Deadly Sins (Scene 6), **Anthony Hooper** (Beelzebub, *left back*), **William Avenell** (Lucifer, *left, well lit*), **Robert Harris** (Faustus, *right*), **Hugh Griffith** (Mephistopheles).
*Photo: Angus McBean*

**3.Hugh Griffith** (Mephistopheles) and **Robert Harris** (Faustus), **Dr Faustus (1946).**
*Photo: Angus McBean*

**4.** Hudd directed **Robert Harris** in the title-role of **Richard II (1947).** The actor was required to wear a special wig for the prison scene. He remembers once '*I nearly dried, and in the process of banging my head to remember the lines, suddenly saw the wig in my hand.*'
**Robert Harris** (Richard II, *centre),* **Donald Sinden** (Aumerle, *left).*
*Photo: Angus McBean*

**Angus McBean** photographer demonstrated the potential of the 'photo-call' and over the next ten years captured the SMT's richness in production and acting talent in a remarkable series of photographs.

49

**proclamation item.**
**That no woman**
**shall come within**
**a mile of my court**

Peter Brook's individual style was first seen at the Memorial Theatre with his **Love's Labour's Lost (1946).** Barry Jackson told Brook *'You are only twenty, so I am giving you a very young man's play. See what you can do with it.'* Brook adopted a Watteau setting with designs by Reginald Leefe and the production became the hit of the season.

**1.** Drop for the Prologue.
*Photo: Daniels*

**2.** Another reason for the production's success was **Paul Scofield**'s interpretation of Don Armado which, according to the critic Philip Hope-Wallace, was *'faintly reminiscent of an over-bred and beautiful old borzoi.'* With **David O'Brien** (Moth).
*Photo: Angus McBean*

**3.** Brook's initial success was followed by a controversial production of **Romeo and Juliet (1947)** in which he cut the Friar Laurence and Juliet 'Potion' scene and the reconciliation of the Montagues and Capulets, — echoing an editorial approach to the original text which had been a hallmark of the 1930's visionary, Komisarjevsky.

Later, Brook defended his approach: '. . . *it is a play of wide spaces in which all scenery and decoration easily become an irrelevance, in which one tree on a bare stage can suggest the loneliness of a place of exile . . . the atmosphere is described in a single line "These hot days is the mad blood stirring", and its treatment must be to capture the violent passion of two children lost among the warring fury of the Southern houses.'*

But the Mail said of the production: '(It was) *a contest of ballet versus the Bard, with the Bard an easy loser.'*

The crenellated city walls were intended to suggest the play's boundaries, and were placed on a red-coloured sand cloth to make the stage blaze with heat and light. Designs by Rolf Gérard. **John Harrison** (Benvolio), **Lawrence Payne** (Romeo).

*Photo: Angus McBean*

# PAUL SCOFIELD

**1.** The directors were blessed by the presence of a group of gifted young actors, led by **Paul Scofield.** As **Henry V (1946)** he was directed by the Bensonian, **Dorothy Green.**

*Photo: Holte*

**2. Scofield** as Oliver in **As You Like It (1946)** directed by **Herbert Prentice,** with **Joy Parker** (Celia), who later became his wife.

*Photo: Angus McBean*

**3. Frank McMullen,** a director/academic from Yale University cast **Scofield** as Lucio in **Measure for Measure (1916);** Scofield squeezed '*all the charm out of the wickedness of the character.*' With **David King Wood** (Duke).

*Photo: Angus McBean*

**4. Scofield** as **Pericles (1947),** the play's first revival since 1900. The director, **Nugent Monck,** cut the play so that it opened with the shipwreck. His object was to '*get the audience in and out and save on the electricity bills.*'

*Photo: Angus McBean*

**5. Scofield** as Aguecheek, in **Twelfth Night (1947)** directed by **Walter Hudd.** He resembled '*a blue and white blancmange*'. (From left to right) **Scofield, Duncan Ross** (Fabian), **Beatrix Lehmann** (Viola) and **John Blatchley** (Sir Toby Belch).

*Photo: Angus McBean*

**6. Anthony Quayle** directed **The Winter's Tale (1948)** with **Paul Scofield** as the Clown and **John Kidd** as the Old Shepherd: '*Tis a lucky day, boy: and we'll do good deeds on't.*'

*Photo: Angus McBean*

## MICHAEL BENTHALL

**1.** Barry Jackson introduced **Michael Benthall,** (who was only 28) to Stratford as a member of the directing team.

*Photo: Angus McBean*

**2.** Benthall's opening play was **King John (1948),** with **Robert Helpmann** *(centre)* in the title-role. Designs by Audrey Cruddas.

*Photo: Angus McBean*

In that same year, Helpmann enjoyed an audience in Rome with Pope Pius XII and mentioned that his current roles included *'Hamlet, and I'm afraid, King John.'* The Pope was unimpressed: *'King John being the first King to denounce the Pope, that is unfortunate.'* 'No,' Helpmann replied, *'It's a very good part, and I'm an actor.'*

**3. Anthony Quayle** doubled as actor. When playing The Bastard in **King John (1948),** (with **Alfie Bass** as his permanent shadow Guerney), Bass remembers that early in the production Quayle forgot his lines, agonising *'Oh God, what's next?'.* The reply, in a whisper: *'Our Father, which art.'*

At the back *(from left to right):* **Ailsa Grahame** (Queen Elinor), **Helpmann** (King John), **Claire Bloom** (Blanche), **Scofield** (Philip of France), **John Justin** (Lewis), **Harold Kasket** (Austria). *Front:* **Quayle** (The Bastard) and **Alfie Bass** (Guerney).

*Photo: Angus McBean*

1. Benthall's 'nineteenth century' production of **Hamlet (1948)**, was the Birthday play of that season. Its novelty derived from casting Paul Scofield and Robert Helpmann to alternate in the title role.

With set and costumes designed by James Bailey, the palace resembled a *'romanticised-Gothic Elsinor'*.

**Scofield** (Hamlet) in the first soliloquy.
*Photo: Angus McBean*

2. **Claire Bloom**, aged 17, made her leading debut in Stratford as their Ophelia. She later confessed *'with each alternately I thought myself in love.'*
*Photo: Angus McBean*

3. The two Hamlets though different were complementary. **Helpmann**'s version was ruled by his *'Falcon eye and penetrating insight so that reason triumphed over blood.'* and he gave a meticulous and balletic performance. . .
*Photo: Angus McBean*

4. . . . while **Scofield's** interpretation was that of a warm-hearted young Prince cut to the heart rather than the brain. His was a romantic, haunted Hamlet; the critic Harold Hobson observed he had *'never seen a Hamlet more shot with the pale agony of irresolution'*.
In the play scene with **Claire Bloom** (Ophelia).

Barry Jackson resigned in 1948, and Benthall and Quayle co-directed most of that season.

**1. The Merchant of Venice (1948)**, (first directed by Benthall in 1947). **Helpmann** was *'an imperious and aristocratic Jew — nothing cringing about him — he made his final exit with his head held high.'* With **Heather Stannard** (Portia).

**2. The Taming of the Shrew (1948)** directed by Michael Benthall, and designed by Rosemary Vercoe in a bizarre concoction of Wild West, eighteenth century and other styles.

**Diana Wynyard** (Katharina), **Anthony Quayle** (Petruchio) and **Alfie Bass** (Grumio, *left*) — *'Fear not, sweet wench, they shall not touch thee, Kate.'*
Photo: Angus McBean

**3. Godfrey Tearle,** son of actor-manager Osmond Tearle, directed, and assumed the title-role of, **Othello (1948).** He gave a performance of *'nobility and simplicity which came from the heart.'*

With *(on the left)* **Anthony Quayle** (Iago) who had persuaded Tearle to join the company.

56

# 5

## The Star-Studded Fifties
## 1949-1959

# ANTHONY QUAYLE

Anthony Quayle succeeded to the directorship at the end of 1948 and became a formidable administrator, widening the international audience for the Theatre with tours to Russia, Australasia, the United States and Europe, and promoting a star system for both guest actors and producers. Quayle invited many senior Shakespearian actors to make their debut at the Memorial Theatre but also encouraged a new generation of home-trained talent.

*All photographs in this chapter, unless otherwise credited, are by Angus McBean.*

**1. Macbeth (1949),** Quayle's first production as Theatre Director, with **Godfrey Tearle** (Macbeth).

**2.** Tearle rejected the actor cast by Anthony Quayle and pointed to the unknown **Jill Bennett**: *'She'll do for Fleance'.* It was the beginning of her *'passionate friendship'* with Godfrey Tearle.

**Leon Quartermaine** (Banquo), **Jill Bennett** (Fleance) in **Macbeth (1949).**

**3.** As Falstaff, Quayle featured in **Glen Byam Shaw's** production of **The Merry Wives of Windsor (1955)** with wintry designs by Motley.

With **Joyce Redman** *(left,* Mistress Ford) and **Angela Baddeley** (Mistress Page).

**4.** In **Byam Shaw's** production of **Troilus and Cressida (1954) Anthony Quayle's** Pandarus was a *'memorable portrait of a lisping, giggling, intriguing old fribble'.* **Muriel Pavlow** (Cressida).

**5. Anthony Quayle's** Aaron, in **Titus Andronicus (1955),** was to be his last major acting role with the SMT.

For the Festival of Britain in 1951, **Anthony Quayle** decided to produce four of Shakespeare's history plays in sequence, from **Richard II** to **Henry V.** This, the first attempt at the cycle since Frank Benson's in 1905, marked the beginning of the epic themes of the histories, which 13 years later produced **John Barton** and **Peter Hall's The Wars of The Roses** and, later still, **Terry Hands' Henry VI** cycle.

Tanya Moiseiwitsch devised a radical and ingenious permanent setting, which would serve all four plays.

**1.** *'Of comfort no man speak'* — **Michael Redgrave** in the title-role of **Richard II (1951)** returns to England to find himself friendless.

**2. Michael Redgrave** played Hotspur in **Henry IV Part 1 (1951)** as an *'impetuous, charming and naïve'* character and omitted the traditional stammer, replacing it with a Northumbrian accent. With **Barbara Jefford** (Lady Percy).

**3.** *'My due from thee is this imperial crown':* at Henry IV's **(Harry Andrews)** deathbed, the young welsh actor, **Richard Burton** (Prince Hal) comes face to face with his destiny in **Henry IV Part 2.** There was a preponderance of Welsh members in the company, so much so that, according to Redgrave, *'the atmosphere of a Rugby final at Cardiff Arms Park was never far away'.*

The critic Harold Hobson considered Burton's Hal to be, *'like a man who has had a private vision of the Holy Grail'.*

**4.** Falstaff's rejection in **Henry IV Part 2 (1951)** with **Anthony Quayle** since hailed as *'one of the great Falstaffs of his generation'.* **Anthony Quayle** (Falstaff), **Richard Wordsworth** (Pistol), **John Gay** (Lancaster), **Richard Burton** (Henry V).

**5.** **Richard Burton** (Henry V) with **Hazel Penwarden** (Katherine).
Burton emerged from the cycle as the dramatic hero as well as the theatrical pin-up of the season, many actresses confessing a more than merely theatrical passion.

**6.** As **Henry V (1951)** *'Richard Burton had an awareness of destiny, of his own fate about him'.* He was shortly to be attracted by the drama of Hollywood. Quayle said of Burton: *'the face was significant and compelling, a magnificent mask. Somebody wrote that "this young man brings on a cathedral in his eyes." Actually what Richard was thinking about was how soon he could get another pint of beer or who . . . But that was a God-sent thing he had, that extraordinary face.'*

60

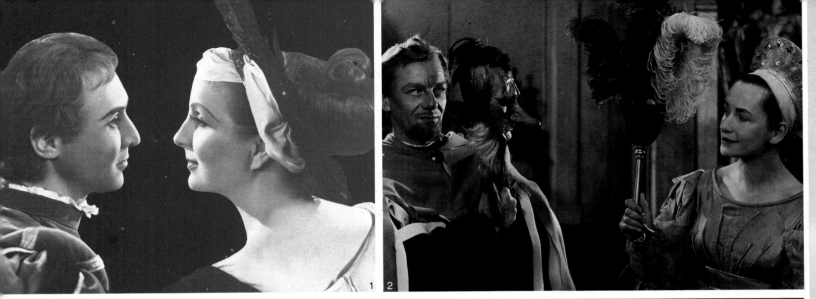

# JOHN GIELGUD

**1.** In Quayle's first year as director he invited John Gielgud to direct **Much Ado About Nothing (1949),** with **Diana Wynyard** and **Quayle** as Beatrice and Benedick. Gielgud commissioned the Spanish artist Mariano Andreu to design the costumes.

**2.** The production was revived the following year (1950) with **Gielgud** both directing and playing Benedick, and **Peggy Ashcroft** as Beatrice. *'Playing opposite Gielgud',* said Peggy Ashcroft, *'was like having a marvellous partner in dance'.*

**3.** Gielgud as Angelo in **Peter Brook's** production of **Measure for Measure (1950).** Portrayed as *'an icy Puritan',* he gave Isabella, the 19-year-old **Barbara Jefford,** *'her baptism of fire'.*

**4.** As Cassius in **Julius Caesar (1950),** co-directed by **Quayle** and **Michael Langham.** Quayle saw Cassius as a *'tough and bitter soldier'.* He accordingly advised Gielgud before rehearsals: *'Go and watch the hard-bitten faces of the men trained for action and responsibility when they come out of the War Office'.*

**John Gielgud** (Cassius), **Harry Andrews** (Brutus).

**5.** Gielgud co-directed **King Lear (1950)** with Quayle, and also played the King as an *'El Greco'* Lear.

**John Gielgud** (Lear), **Alan Badel** (Fool).

**1. Gwen Ffrangcon-Davies** (Regan) found **Peggy Ashcroft's** Cordelia so moving that she was *'moved to guilty tears . . . not at all what I was supposed to be feeling'*.

**John Gielgud** (Lear), **Peggy Ashcroft** (Cordelia), **Paul Hardwick** (Cornwall), **Gwen Ffrangcon-Davies** (Regan), **Michael Gwynn** (Albany), **Maxine Audley** (Goneril) in **King Lear (1950)**.

**2. John Gielgud** and **George Devine** co-directed a stylised production of **King Lear (1955)**, designed by the Japanese sculptor, Isamu Noguchi. (For Emlyn Williams, *'a sort of Gipsy Rose Lear'*). JC Trewin considered Lear's headress was *'an inverted hatstand'* and Punch commented, *'no wonder Lear left a home in which he had to sit side saddle on an abstract horse.'*

**Helen Cherry** (Goneril), **John Gielgud** (Lear), **Claire Bloom** (Cordelia), **Moira Lister** (Regan).

**3. The Tempest (1957)**. **Richard Johnson** recalls that during Prospero's final soliloquy Gielgud's eyes *'were gradually spouting tears'* — a reference to Gielgud's facility with the famous *'Terry tears'*.

**Brian Bedford** (Ariel), **Richard Johnson** (Ferdinand), **John Gielgud** (Propero).

**4. Peter Brook** directed and designed this *Tempest* and composed the *musique concrète*. The island's scenery and vegetation was described as *'a proper obstacle race of hanging fronds'* in which *'the clowning was uninhibited'*.

**Clive Revill** (Trinculo), **Alec Clunes** (Caliban), **Patrick Wymark** (Stephano).

# TYRONE GUTHRIE

**Michael Blakemore** (then an actor) remembers the famous director, Guthrie turning up *'to rehearse each day in the same old clothes and on his feet battered plimsolls — without socks. This immensely tall figure looked like an arctic explorer in retirement, or a brigadier with a passion for something unexpected, like needlework'.*

**1.** Guthrie staged an acclaimed production of **Henry VIII (1950)** with an innovative, permanent set designed by Tanya Moiseiwitsch and soldiers borrowed from the local Royal Warwickshire Regiment.

**Andrew Cruickshank** (Wolsey, *left),* **Anthony Quayle** (Henry), **Gwen Ffrangcon-Davies** (Katherine), **Robert Hardy** (Griffith, *right of steps).*

**2.** Guthrie returned to direct **All's Well That Ends Well (1959)** — his last great British production. **Michael Blakemore** (Dumain, *far left)* recalls that Guthrie *'treated the spear-carriers like stars and stars like spear-carriers'.* Guthrie's crowd scenes *'. . .were famous because there were no crowds: instead clusters of individuals milling and dispersing at the service of the narrative'.* In the war scene, set in the African desert, some were reminded of TV's *The Army Game.*

**Edward de Souza** *(brandishing sword,* Bertram), **Paul Hardwick** (Longaville, *on Bertram's left),* **Cyril Luckham** (Parolles, *blindfold),* **Peter Woodthorpe** (First Soldier, *drinking* ).

**3. Edith Evans** (Countess of Rousillon) in the same production.

## GLEN BYAM SHAW

In 1952 Quayle invited Glen Byam Shaw to join him as co-director of the SMT. And from 1957-59 he replaced Quayle as the Theatre's director.

**1. Marius Goring** in the title-role in **Richard III (1953)**: *'nasty not evil'*.

*Photo: Holte*

**2. Laurence Harvey** and **Zena Walker** (age 20) as the lovers in **Romeo and Juliet (1954).**

**3.** Byam Shaw invited **Michael Langham** to direct **Alan Badel** as **Hamlet (1956)** with **Diana Churchill** (Gertrude), **Harry Andrews** (Claudius), **George Howe** *(far right,* Polonius).

**4.** He also asked **Noel Willman** to direct **All's Well That Ends Well (1955).** **Edward Atienza** (Lavache) *'spent hours before the performance squatting on a spike which was attached to his bottom, while he invented a variety of poses to satisfy his conception of the part'.* With **Keith Michell** (Parolles).

**5. Dorothy Tutin's** first play at the Memorial Theatre was **Romeo and Juliet (1958).** She was terrified and remembers Byam Shaw's advice, *'Don't forget, use your nerves'.*

**Angela Baddeley** (Nurse), **Dorothy Tutin** (Juliet), **Richard Johnson** (Romeo).

## GEORGE DEVINE

In 1952 Quayle also asked George Devine to direct at the SMT. He directed five productions between 1952-5 before leaving to establish the Royal Court Theatre in London. These included:

1. **Volpone (1952)** which was added to the 1952 season at Ralph Richardson's request, became a *'romping production'* in which Anthony Quayle's Mosca was described as *'splendidly devious and oilily parasitical'*.

**Ralph Richardson** (Volpone), **Anthony Quayle** (Mosca).

2. **Tony Britton** (Lysander) and **Zena Walker** (Hermia) in Devine's production of **A Midsummer Night's Dream (1954),** designed by Motley.

3. **Leo McKern** describes the part of Quince in the same production as a most joyful thing, *'apart from the fortunately brief period when Tony Quayle's Bottom, in an excess of health-food enthusiasm took to chewing raw garlic'*.

**Mervyn Blake** (Snug), **Ian Bannen** (Flute), **Leo McKern** (Quince), **Anthony Quayle** (Bottom), **James Grout** (Snout), **Peter Duguid** (Starveling).

**Keith Michell** (Petruchio), **Beverley Cross** (Gregory), **Barbara Jefford** (Katherina), **Ian Bannen** (Curtis), **Kevin Miles** Nathaniel).

4. **Barbara Jefford** (Katherina) in Devine's **The Taming of the Shrew (1954)** recalls the director's method of keeping the comedy within bounds in rehearsals: he employed a *'pop-gun ... which he used with great accuracy to bounce corks off heads of any offending comics within range'*.

5. In 1955, Devine himself played Dogberry in **Gielgud's** production of **Much Ado About Nothing.**

# MICHAEL REDGRAVE

Michael Redgrave lent weight to a number of major roles:

1. As Prospero in **Michael Benthall's** production of **The Tempest (1951).** Designer Loudon Sainthill used 102 candles, so that the floor was covered with wax by the end of each performance.

**Alan Badel** (Ariel, *left at back)*, **Geoffrey Bayldon** (Gonzalo), **Alan Townsend** (Francisco), **Jack Gwillim** (Alonso), **Michael Redgrave** (Prospero), **William Squire** (Sebastian), **Brendon Barry** (Adrian), **William Fox** (Antonio).

2. In that production, **Geoffrey Bayldon** recalls one of the earliest uses of dry ice. In one performance, it was lavished to such an extent that it camouflaged the entire set — but not all the cast objected to being hidden. Richard Burton confided of his part in the production, *'I felt like a (expletive deleted!) pink meringue.'*

**Richard Burton** (Ferdinand), **Hazel Penwarden** (Miranda), **Barbara Jefford** (Juno, *on cloud)*

3. As Shylock with **Yvonne Mitchell** (Jessica) in a production by **Denis Carey** (a guest producer from the Bristol Old Vic) of **The Merchant of Venice (1953).**

Redgrave's Shylock was not played for sympathy: *'His eyes bulge. . . His arms semaphore. . . a man possessed with the devil which stubbornly refuses to be cast out,'* said Kenneth Tynan.

7

8

**4.** As **King Lear (1953)** in **George Devine's** production, with **Marius Goring** (Fool).

**5.** Michael Redgrave played **Hamlet (1958)** at 50. The production travelled to Moscow where the spy, Guy Burgess, made a drunken visit backstage, a story later adapted by Alan Bennett in his television play, *An Englishman Abroad.*

**6. Michael Redgrave** (Hamlet), **Dorothy Tutin** (Ophelia), **Hamlet (1958).**

**7. Googie Withers** (Gertrude) also in **Hamlet (1958)** at Stratford recalls *'I couldn't remember my first line. Panic set in — I called out . . . — 'My line! My line! For God's sake what is my line?' Suddenly a voice came from the flies, in a strong Warwickshire accent, and said — "One woe doth tread upon another's 'eels, so fast they follow". Where else in the world would one get a Shakespearian prompt from a stage hand?'* (Coral Browne played Gertrude in Moscow).

**8.** Michael Redgrave as Benedick in **Douglas Searle's Much Ado About Nothing (1958).** The play was given an early Victorian setting with music and dancing; but a member of the audience is reported to have objected to this 'Shakespearian waltzing'. With **Googie Withers** (Beatrice).

5

# THE OLIVIERS

Both Laurence Olivier and his wife Vivien Leigh, promised **Glen Byam Shaw** that they would *'assist'* at his 10th season. Despite their fame, they *'insisted to be treated as modest members of the ensemble'*.

**1.** They opened in **Twelfth Night (1955)** under the direction of John Gielgud. Olivier's unorthodox Malvolio was described as an *'underweening Roundhead among Cavaliers'*.

**Vivien Leigh** (Viola), **Laurence Olivier** (Malvolio).

**2. Twelfth Night (1955):** **Laurence Olivier** (Malvolio), **Michael Denison** (Aguecheek), **Alan Webb** (Sir Toby Belch), **Angela Baddeley** (Maria), **Lee Montagu** (Fabian).

**3. Emrys James** (who had first joined the SMT in 1955) recalled one occasion during the rehearsals for **Twelfth Night (1955):** *'Olivier's gutsy theatricality. . . went too far for Gielgud's sensibility . . . when Olivier as Malvolio climbed out of the prison he rummaged in his costume and produced first a handful of mud, then a bunch of hay and finally a dead rat.'*

**Maxine Audley** (Olivia), **Trader Faulkner** (Sebastian), **Lee Montagu** (Fabian), **Laurence Olivier** (Malvolio), **Keith Michell** (Orsino), **Vivien Leigh** (Viola).

**4. Olivier** as **Macbeth (1955)** under the direction of Glen Byam Shaw, opposite **Vivien Leigh** (Lady Macbeth). He

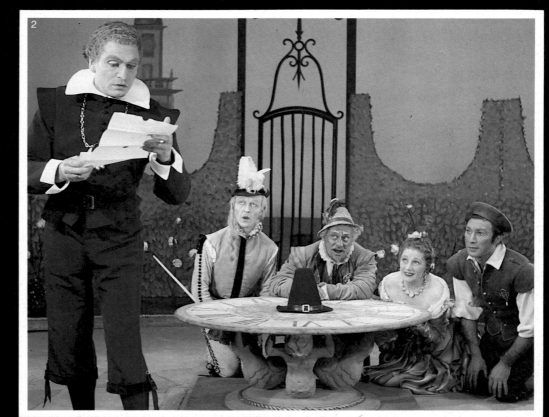

recalls, in his recent autobiography, Sybil Thorndike saying *'You must be married to play the Macbeths'.*

**5. Vivien Leigh** (Lady Macbeth) *'red-haired, green-gowned, exquisite of speech'* in **Macbeth (1955).**

**6. Laurence Olivier's Macbeth (1955)** demonstrating his swordsmanship against **Keith Michell** (Macduff). The play is notorious for mishaps. The actor, Ralph Michael, recalls the mountainside fight when *'from a prone position below stage I saw Olivier's woollen tights do the splits, as a cascade of flagons bombarded me, the scenery became uncleated, and Olivier swung perilously towards the auditorium, until saved by the strong right arm of his adversary. . .'*

**Keith Michell** (Macduff), **Laurence Olivier** (Macbeth).

By the time Macbeth had opened, Vivien Leigh had hosted numerous parties late into the night and life in Stratford had become one huge social whirl; the box office was overwhelmed.

**7. Titus Andronicus (1955),** with *Olivier* in the *'punishing role',* and **Vivien Leigh** as Lavinia. This was the first production at the SMT of this play, with its *'thirteen deaths, two mutilations, a rape and a cannibal feast'.* Peter Brook edited and directed the play, and also designed the costumes and musical effects. The critic Bernard Levin described Olivier's Titus as *'not so much on the heroic scale as on a new scale entirely, the greatness of which has smashed all our measuring-rods and pressure gauges to smithereens'.*

# PEGGY ASHCROFT

The Fifties saw the beginning of Peggy Ashcroft's close association with Stratford. Already a distinguished actress (she was created a Dame in 1956) she first played at the SMT as Beatrice (see above).

**1.** As Portia in **The Merchant of Venice (1953).**

**2.** In 1957, **Glen Byam Shaw** persuaded Peggy Ashcroft, then 49, to play Rosalind in his production of **As You Like It,** opposite the young **Richard Johnson** (Orlando). The critics were unanimous in their praise: *'she made nonsense of arithmetic: miraculously youthful, light and eager'* (WA Darlington, Daily Telegraph); *'At once boyish and womanly,'* said Philip Hope-Wallace, and Richard Johnson found her generous and supportive.

**3.** The final dance scene in **As You Like It (1957),** showing Motley's spring designs.

**Robert Arnold** (Silvius), **Patrick Wymark** (Touchstone), **Stephanie Bidmead** (Audrey), **Peggy Ashcroft** (Rosalind), **Richard Johnson** (Orlando), **Robin Lloyd** (Oliver), **Doreen Aris** (Phebe), **Jane Wenham** (Celia).

**4.** In Byam Shaw's successful production of **Antony and Cleopatra (1953), Peggy Ashcroft** starred as a controversial Cleopatra, with a red pony-tail and fair skin. The production *'came nearer to perfection than any in living memory,'* and transferred to London.

**Michael Redgrave** (Antony), **Peggy Ashcroft** (Cleopatra).

1

2

3

4

## INTERNATIONAL GUEST STARS

By invitation, actors and directors from overseas helped to establish the SMT as an internationally pre-eminent theatre.

**1. Tony Richardson's** production of **Othello (1959)** featured **Paul Robeson** in the title-role, which he had played previously in London and America, and **Mary Ure** (then John Osborne's wife) as Desdemona.
> *photo: Tony Armstrong Jones*

**2. Othello (1959)** featured two American actors, **Sam Wanamaker** (Iago) and **Paul Robeson** (Othello).
> *Photo: Tony Armstrong Jones*

**3. Tony Richardson** also directed **Pericles (1958)** with **Edric Connor** as *'a calypso-singing Gower'* (centre).

**4. Charles Laughton**, by now an international film star, played the lead in **King Lear (1959)** in **Glen Byam Shaw's** last Stratford production, with **Albert Finney** (Edgar), **Anthony Nicholls** (Kent) and *(far right)* **Ian Holm** (Fool).

# PETER HALL

**1.** Both Quayle and Glen Byam Shaw had noted the talented work of **Peter Hall**, then a 24-year-old Cambridge graduate, and agreed to assign him his first Stratford production — **Love's Labour's Lost (1956)**, co-incidentally the first play directed by Peter Brook when he joined the SMT under Barry Jackson.

**Geraldine McEwan** (Princess of France), **Alan Badel** (Berowne), **Greta Watson** (Katharine), **Dilys Hamlett** (Maria), **Jeannette Sterke** (Rosaline).

**2. Clive Revill** (Costard), **Richard O'Sullivan** (Moth), **Harry Andrews** (Don Armado) in the same production.

**3.** Hall directed **Cymbeline (1957),** designed by the distinguished Italian painter Lila de Nobili. It was also his first meeting with **Peggy Ashcroft** (Imogen).

**4. Geraldine McEwan** (Olivia) **Dorothy Tutin** (Viola) in **Peter Hall's** Caroline production of **Twelfth Night (1958)**.

**5. Patrick Wymark** (Sir Toby Belch) **Ian Richardson** (Aguecheek) in **Twelfth Night (1960)**.

6. Hall's **A Midsummer's Night Dream (1959)** was directed as a *'wedding revel in a lordly Tudor home'* where **Charles Laughton's** Bottom *'loomed and bulged at the centre of things: without being the tyrant of the mummings'*...

7. *'...while the young fairies were magnetic and impudent'*. **Ian Holm** (Puck) was a *'pert piece of mischief'* with *(top right)* **Robert Hardy** (Oberon), **Edward de Souza** (Demetrius), **Albert Finney** (Lysander), **Vanessa Redgrave** (Helena), **Priscilla Morgan** (Hermia).

8. Peter Hall's **Coriolanus (1959)** showed how far Anthony Quayle's hopes for the SMT had been fulfilled: Stratford attracted well-known actors, promising new talent and a new generation of directors.

**Edith Evans** (Volumnia) was described as having the *'heart as well as the hauteur'* of the character. With **Vanessa Redgrave** (Valeria) and **Mary Ure** (Virgilia).

9. **Olivier** in the title-role of **Coriolanus (1959).**

# 6

## The Radical
## Sixties
## 1960-1967

**Peter Hall** effectively became Director of the SMT from 1960. During the next eight years he redesigned the Stratford stage (it was raked and extended further into the auditorium, with seats on either side); raised the Theatre's first subsidy after *'eighty years of self-sufficiency':* in 1961, changed its name to 'The Royal Shakespeare Theatre'; and founded a company, the Royal Shakespeare Company, which played in both Stratford and London (at the Aldwych Theatre). His aim was to expand the role of the Theatre to work both in classical and modern drama: *'My heritage is made up of photos and legends . . . I hope to create a style which is recognizable and Stratford's own, and to reinterpret the plays in terms of that style. To do this I shall need a company that remains basically, though not entirely, the same . . . My plans are very ambitious.'* The legacy of Hall's structure is still in place today.

His two-theatre policy resulted in a Stratford season, with emphasis on Shakespeare, from April to December, and a London season presenting a programme of modern works and other classics. Peter Hall hoped that it could be possible for *'. . . an actor to play Shakespeare in Stratford on Monday and John Whiting in London on Tuesday'.*

**Peter Hall, Peter Brook** and **Michel Saint-Denis.**

*Photo: Gordon Goode*

75

# LONDON

**1.** The Aldwych Theatre exterior, 1960.
*Photo: Angus McBean*

**2.** At the end of 1960, **The Duchess of Malfi** by John Webster opened the Company's first Aldwych season. The production, directed by **Donald McWhinnie,** included **Peggy Ashcroft,** who became a founder-member of the RSC (she is still an Associate Artist and, in 1968, joined its Directorate). Success was immediate: '. . . *the first London performance of a national repertory company . . . which will rank eventually with the Comédie Francaise, the Berliner Ensemble and the Moscow Art Theatre.'*

**Max Adrian** (Cardinal), **Eric Porter** (Ferdinand), **Peggy Ashcroft** (Duchess of Malfi), **Donald Douglas** (Grisolan), **Clifford Rose** (Silvio).
*Photo: Angus McBean*

**3. The Cherry Orchard (1961)** by Chekhov, in a version by John Gielgud, was directed by **Michel Saint-Denis** (who, together with Peter Brook, joined the artistic directorate in 1962).

**Dorothy Tutin** (Varya), **Peggy Ashcroft** (Madame Ranevsky), **Judi Dench** (Anya).
*Photo: John Timbers*

**4. The Beggar's Opera (1963)** by John Gay was directed by **Peter Wood.**

**Tony Church** (Lockit), **Patience Collier** (Mrs Trapes), **Ronald Radd** (Peachum).
*Photo: Zoë Dominic*

**6**

### Royal Shakespeare in Danger

Sir — There is a great danger that the Royal Shakespeare Company may have to cease its London productions. . . unless the company is given either an immediate grant of public money or at least the firm promise of one very soon.

As dramatic critics we have sometimes differed among ourselves as to the merits of individual productions by the company. But we would like to affirm, unanimously, our belief in the vital importance of the company to the life of the London theatre. . .

Felix Barker, Alan Brien, W.A. Darlington, Bamber Gascoigne, Harold Hobson, Philip Hope-Wallace, Bernard Levin, Robert Muller, Milton Shulman, Kenneth Tynan, T.C. Worsley, London EC4.

**5. The Caucasian Chalk Circle (1962)** by Brecht, the RSC's first Brecht production, was directed by **William Gaskill** and designed by Ralph Koltai.

**Michael Flanders** (Arkadi), **Eric Flyn, Sebastian Breaks, Derek Newark** (Iron Troopers), **Hugh Griffith** (Azdak), **Declan Mulholland** (Schauwa).

*Photo: Reg Wilson*

**6.** Hall's new season at the Aldwych broke with the Company tradition by commissioning plays from such dramatists as John Arden, Robert Bolt, Peter Shaffer and John Whiting. Under the influence of both **Peter Brook** and **Michel Saint-Denis** the Arts Theatre was used in 1962 for experimental and European drama. State subsidy also made it possible for Peter Hall to exercise his flair for innovative contemporary works. The case for public funding generated considerable publicity (see letter to Daily Telegraph, 9 July 1962).

**7. The Devils (1961)** by John Whiting was the first play commissioned by the RSC. The production was directed by **Peter Wood.** Judged by many critics a masterpiece, it was revived the following year.

**Richard Johnson** (Grandier).

*Photos: Reg Wilson*

**The Devils (1962) Peter McEnery** (de Laubardemont), **Max Adrian** (Father Barre), **Dorothy Tutin** (Sister Jeanne), **Alan Dobie** (Prince Henri de Conde).

**1. & 2.** One of the experimental new plays included David Rudkin's **Afore Night Come (1962),** directed by **Clifford Williams** (his first RSC production).

'*. . . not since* Look Back In Anger *has a playwright made a debut more striking than this*' said Kenneth Tynan. The Lord Chamberlain (the official Dramatic Censor until 1968) insisted on 34 cuts: (see letter).

*(Left to right)* **Joe Gibbons** (Albert), **David Warner** (Jim, *foreground crouching*), **Peter McEnery** (Johnny Hobnails), **Henley Thomas** (Jeff), **Gerry Duggan** (Roche), **Henry Woolf** (Tiny), **Timothy West** (Ginger).

**Peter McEnery** (Johnny Hobnails), **Henry Woolf** (Tiny).
*Photos: Reg Wilson*

Plays by foreign dramatists included:

**3. Becket or the Honour of God (1961)** by Jean Anouilh directed by **Peter Hall** with **Eric Porter** (Becket), **Christopher Plummer** (King Henry).
*Photo: Angus McBean*

**4. Clifford Williams'** British premiere of the controversial anti-papist play **The Representative (1963)** by Rolf Hochhuth. **Michael Williams** (Eichmann) recalls *'there was a phone call with the message "we're going to get you" . . . six fellas turned up at the stage door during the curtain call and I got police protection from Bow Street for the run of the play.'*

**Alan Webb** (Pope Pius XII). **Alec McCowen** (Riccardo Fontana),
*Photo: Reg Wilson .*

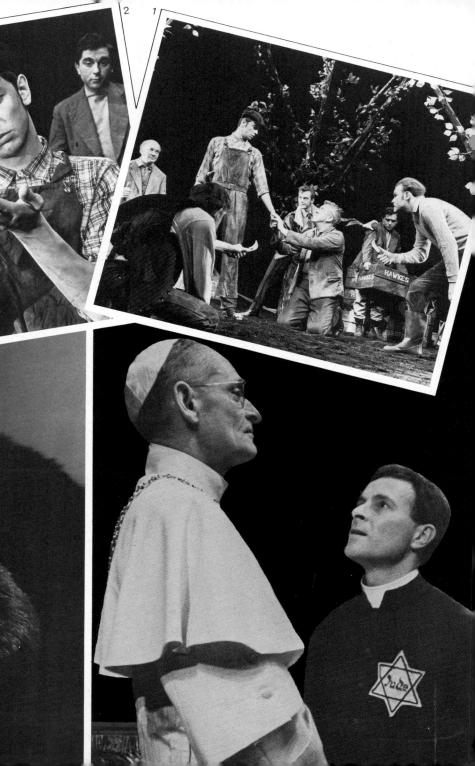

**5. The Physicists (1963)** by Dürrenmatt, directed by **Peter Brook** and **Robert David MacDonald.**

At table, **Michael Hordern** (Beutler/Newton), **Cyril Cusack** (Möbius), **Alan Webb** (Ernesti/Einstein). Standing, **Kenneth Gardnier** (McArthur), **Tony Steedman** (Uwe Sievers), **Jonathan Holdern** (Murillo).

*Photos 5-6: Reg Wilson*

**6. The Criminals (1967)** by José Triana was **Terry Hands'** directorial debut at the Aldwych.

**Brenda Bruce** (Cuca), **Barrie Ingham** (Lalo).

The Company's reputation for experimental work was boosted by the 1964 'Theatre of Cruelty' season at the Lamda Theatre Studio under **Peter Brook** and **Charles Marowitz.** This was followed by a series of plays at the Aldwych which provoked critical acclaim and controversy in what came to be known as the 'dirty plays' season.

**7.** Peter Weiss' **Marat-Sade (1964)** directed by **Peter Brook** (full-title, 'The Persecution and Assassination of Marat as performed by the Inmates of the Asylum of Charenton under the Direction of the Marquis de Sade'). The play was an *'experiment in lunacy'* and provided strong meat for audiences and actors alike. *'One wasn't quite able to cope with one's own inner violences and nastiness'* . . .' said actor **Morgan Sheppard.**

*(Foreground left to right):* **Patrick Magee** (de Sade), **Glenda Jackson** (Charlotte Corday), **Clive Revill** (Marat).

*Photo: Morris Newcombe*

**Michael Williams** recalls when the production transferred to

New York there were fights for tickets. *'On one occasion a couple of students were found on stage under the sunken baths so they could see the show. During the first night the NY audience went uncharacteristically quiet; they were terrified that the mad people would go into the auditorium'.* In his review for The Observer, Bamber Gascoigne said, *'As an experiment, Peter Brook's "Theatre of Cruelty" at Lamda now proves its worth.'*

**1.** In 1966, **Peter Brook** devised with **Denis Cannan** a production criticising the American involvement in Vietnam: **US**, the outcome of a four-month rehearsal period, was presented at the Aldwych and was destined to bring the RSC into the political arena: *'...detachment is finally broken down. I have never before experienced this so fully in a theatre ...'* said the critic of The Times.

Roles were played by the company as an *ensemble*.

*Photo: Reg Wilson*

**Peter Hall** directed several new plays, including:

**2.** The RSC's first Pinter play, **The Collection (1962)**, initially at the Arts Theatre with **John Ronane** (Bill), **Michael Hordern** (Harry).

*Photo: Zoë Dominic*

**3.** Pinter's third full-length play **The Homecoming (1965)**, designed, as was *The Collection*, by John Bury. The production won several awards.

**John Normington** (Sam), **Paul Rogers** (Max), **Terence Rigby** (Joey), **Ian Holm** (Lenny), **Michael Craig** (Teddy).

*Photo: David Sim*

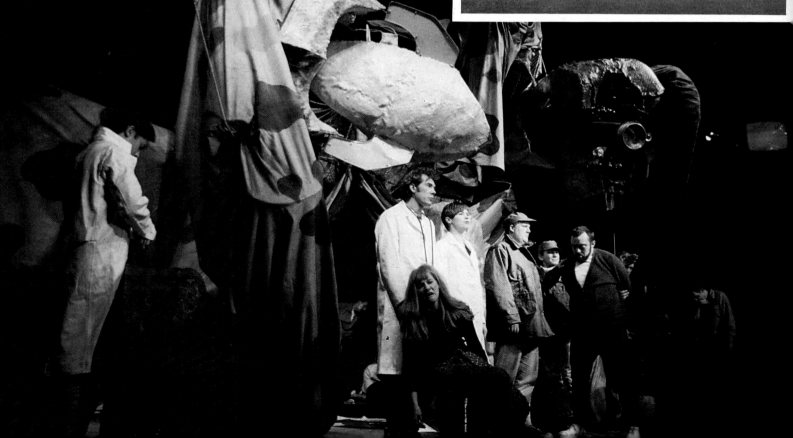

**4. The Government Inspector (1966)** by Gogol, adapted by Jeremy Brooks.

*Front row:* **Patsy Byrne** (Mayor's daughter), **Paul Rogers** (Mayor), **Paul Scofield** (Khlestakov), **Patience Collier** (Mayor's wife). *Back row:* **Ted Valentine** (Superintendent), **Terence Greenidge** (Physician), **John Kane** (Mishka), **Jeffery Dench** (Fistov), **Tim Wylton** (Bobchinsky).

*Photo: Reg Wilson*

**5. Staircase (1966)** by Charles Dyer.

**Patrick Magee** (Harry Leeds), **Paul Scofield** (Charles Dyer).

*Photo: Zoë Dominic*

**6.** In 1960, **John Barton** joined the Company as Associate Director, with special responsibility for verse-speaking.

*Photo: Erich Hartmann-Mangnum*

**Emrys James** recalls some of Barton's *'peculiar rehearsal habits — like chewing razor blades; falling backwards off the stage while providing a perfect illustration of an iambic pentameter and not breaking the flow of the rhythm while he fell. Sometimes he would get his foot caught in the large tins we used as ashtrays. But nothing disturbed his absorption with the verse and the text.'* Barton devised and took part in **The Hollow Crown (1960),** an anthology of words and music about the Kings and Queens of England. It was originally intended as a one-off *'divertissement',* but since has toured worldwide to international acclaim with Company members.

# . . .STRATFORD

At Stratford, the productions gradually became simpler in design, and the star system declined, as Hall encouraged home-bred talent.

**1. The Merchant of Venice (1960),** directed by **Michael Langham** with designs by Desmond Heeley.

**Patrick Wymark** (Gratiano), **Dorothy Tutin** (Portia), **Patrick Allen** (Antonio), **Denholm Elliott** (Bassanio), **Peter O'Toole** (Shylock).

*Photos 1-5: Angus McBean*

**2. The Taming of The Shrew (1960)** was **John Barton's** first production at Stratford, as well as the first time **Peggy Ashcroft** played Katharina of which she said, *'A very stimulating, rather dangerous adventure! But ... intensely enjoyable'.*
With **Peter O'Toole** (Petruchio).

**3.** The same season featured **Peggy Ashcroft** in **The Winter's Tale (1960).**

**Peggy Ashcroft** (Paulina), **Paul Hardwick** (Camillo), **Elizabeth Sellars** (Hermione), **Eric Porter** (Leontes), **Patrick Allen** (Polixenes).

**4.** The production was directed by **Peter Wood.**

**Dennis Waterman** (Mamillius), **Ian Richardson** (2nd Old Gentleman), **Roy Dotrice** (1st Old Gentleman), **Maroussia Frank** (2nd Lady-in-Waiting), **Diana Rigg** (Lady), **Mavis Edwards** (Emilia).

**5. Troilus and Cressida (1960)** was directed by **Peter Hall** and **John Barton**, who also staged the fights.

**Derek Godfrey** (Hector), **Patrick Allen** (Achilles).

4

**6.** The production was also notable for Leslie Hurry's stark set designs.

**William Wallis** (Servant), **Clive Swift** (Helenus, *seated left*), **Clifford Rose** (Priam, *on throne*), **Dave Thomas** (Attendant, *standing*), **Don Webster** (Deiphobus, *seated front*), **Derek Godfrey** (Hector), **Roger Bizley** (Margarelon), **Denholm Elliott** (Troilus), **David Sumner** (Paris).

*Photo: Angus McBean*

**7.** A new generation of younger actors was given leading roles during the Sixties: **Michael Elliott's** production of **As You Like It (1961)** was *'lit up'* by **Vanessa Redgrave's** Rosalind, with **Ian Bannen** as Orlando.

*Photo: Zoë Dominic*

**8.** Richard III (1961) introduced **Christopher Plummer** (in the title-role) to Stratford, and was directed by **William Gaskill** with designs by Jocelyn Herbert.

*Photo: Angus McBean*

**9.** Established actors still continued to feature alongside the new talent:

**Edith Evans** (Nurse) in **Peter Hall's Romeo and Juliet (1961).**

*Photo: Angus McBean*

Modern stage effects (in particular, the revolving stage), were not without their drawbacks: **Tony Church** (Chorus) recalls **Edith Evans** was *'revolved by mistake into the middle of Friar Laurence's cell: Max Adrian (Friar) pauses, blesses her, she curtsies, exits, and he finishes his couplet'.*

83

**1. Hall** revived his celebrated production of **A Midsummer Night's Dream (1962),** first seen in Stratford in 1959. The 1962 production was later used as the basis for both television and film productions.

**Judi Dench** (Titania, *left),* **Nerys Hughes** (Fairy).

*Photos 1-4: Gordon Goode*

Judi Dench remembers it as *'a sensational production . . . one of the most beautiful that I'd ever seen. Lila de Nobili's costumes were exquisite, and the wigs were made from yak hair from Paris. On one occasion during the lullaby scene, Nerys was combing this yak hair when suddenly the brush got stuck in the wig and I spent the rest of the performance with the brush in my hair'.*

**2. Measure For Measure (1962)** directed by **John Blatchley** opened the very successful 1962 season.

**Judi Dench** (Isabella), **Marius Goring** (Angelo).

**3. Cymbeline (1962),** directed by **William Gaskill** with **Vanessa Redgrave** (Imogen), **Eric Porter** (Iachimo).

Eric Porter remembers being taken by surprise at the sight of *'a mole Vanessa Redgrave had painted on her breast for the First Night'.*

**4. The Comedy of Errors (1962)** received only a three-week rehearsal from **Clifford Williams** — his first Stratford production. Introduced as a stopgap, it became an outstanding success and was repeated annually until 1965 and revived in 1972.

Kenneth Tynan noted *'With its few props The Comedy of Errors is unmistakably an RSC production . . . Peter Hall's troupe has developed . . . a classical style of its own. How is it to be recognised? By solid Brechtian settings that emphasize wood and metal instead of paint and canvas . . .'*

**Tony Steedman** (Solinus), **Ian Hewitson** (Dromio of Ephesus), **John Corvin** (Officer), **Ian Richardson** (Antipholus of Ephesus), **Pauline Letts** (Aemilia), **Diana Rigg** (Adriana), **Tony Church** (Aegeon), **Barry MacGregor** (Dromio of Syracuse), **Susan Maryott** (Luciana), **Alec McCowen** (Antipholus of Syracuse).

**5.** This radical approach to Shakespearian production reached its apogee with **Peter Brook's** minimalist **King Lear (1962).** Reminiscent of his earlier *Romeo and Juliet,* it was regarded as one of the first *'bare stage'* RSC productions. Brook followed the Quarto text rather than the Folio or later, more traditionally used editions. It was the first obvious use of comparitive textual readings in the RSC's approach to the plays. Subsequently, the production toured Europe, the USA and Soviet Union and, in 1968, was made into a film.

**Patience Collier** (Regan), **Tony Church** (Cornwall), **Hugh Sullivan** (France), **Paul Scofield** (Lear), **Tony Steedman** (Burgundy), **Diana Rigg** (Cordelia), **Peter Jeffrey** (Albany), **Irene Worth** (Goneril).
*Photo: Angus McBean*

# THE HISTORY CYCLE

Visual spareness was complemented by a new approach to verse speaking. **John Barton** dissected the language, adopting a *'rational style'*.

The artistic and technical collaboration peaked with the history cycle of **The Wars of The Roses (1963),** in which **John Barton** condensed the *Henry VI* trilogy and *Richard III* into three plays: **"Henry VI"**, **"Edward IV"** and **"Richard III".** The following year, to mark Shakespeare's Quartercentenary, the history plays from **Richard II** to **Henry V** were added, so that Shakespeare's complete cycle of the main history plays was presented for the first time. Hall's and Barton's objective was to reflect the current political and social times. The seven plays were directed by **Peter Hall** with **John Barton, Clifford Williams, Peter Wood** and **Frank Evans** as co-directors. The designer, John Bury, featured a central *'steel image',* reinforcing the unity of theme, acting and direction and Guy Woolfenden composed the music throughout. The project bore witness to the success of Hall's ambition to create an ensemble company of actors, directors and designers. He had, said Bernard Levin, created *'a landmark and a beacon in the post-war English theatre, a triumphant vindication of Mr Hall's policy, as well as his power as a producer'.*

*All photos by Gordon Goode unless otherwise credited.*

**1. The Wars of The Roses, Part 1 (1963).** David Warner (Henry VI) with **Peggy Ashcroft** (Queen Margaret). Ashcroft played Margaret throughout the cycle, from a 16-year-old through to the mad Margaret of *Richard III*.

**2. The Wars of The Roses, Part 1 (1963).** Janet Suzman (Joan la Pucelle), **Donald Sinden** (York, *left)*.

**3. The Wars of The Roses, Part 2 (1963).** David Warner (Henry VI), **Donald Sinden** (York), **Brewster Mason** (Warwick).

**4. The Wars of The Roses, Part 3 (1963).** Ian Holm (Richard III).

*Photo: Tom Holte*

**5. The Wars of The Roses, Part 3 (1963).** Tom Fleming (Buckingham), **Peggy Ashcroft** (Margaret).

**6. The Wars of The Roses, Part 3 (1963).** Derek Waring (Richmond), **Ian Holm** (Richard III) in the final scene of this cycle: The Battle of Bosworth.

**1. Roy Dotrice,** (Hotspur, *centre),* in **Henry IV, Part 1 (1964).**

**2. Patience Collier** (Mistress Quickly), **Hugh Griffith** (Falstaff) in **Henry IV, Part 2 (1964).**

**3. Donald Layne-Smith** (Bishop of Ely, *studying book),* **Charles Kay** (Archbishop of Canterbury), **Ian Holm** (Henry V), **Donald Burton** (Exeter), **Anthony Boden**(Gloucester), **Keith James** (Bedford), **David Lyn** (Cambridge) in **Henry V (1964).**

*Photo: Tom Holte*

**4. David Warner** in the title-role of **Richard II (1964).**

*Photo: Reg Wilson*

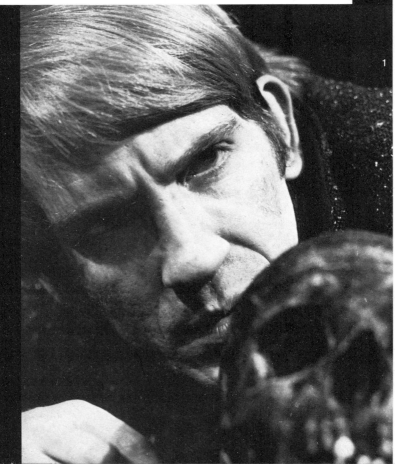

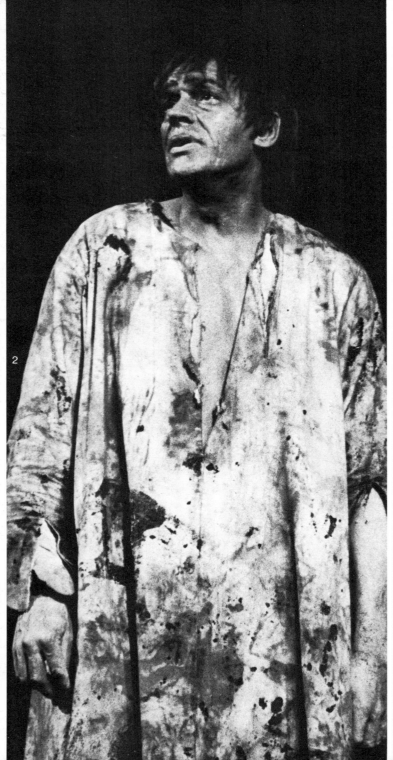

Other notable Stratford productions of the period included:

**1. Peter Hall's Hamlet (1965)** with **David Warner** as an alienated 1960s adolescent Prince, echoing the apathy of his generation. Warner became a 'cult' figure for the younger members of the audience and was mobbed by fans at the end of each performance.

*Photo: Reg Wilson*

**2. John Schlesinger's** production of **Timon of Athens (1965)** boasted a fine central performance from **Paul Scofield** as Timon.

For **Michael Williams** (Painter), Scofield's performance made him aware of *'the greatness in acting which can be there unconsciously.'*

*Photos 2-3: Gordon Goode*

**3. Clifford Williams** directed Marlowe's **The Jew of Malta (1965)** back-to-back with **The Merchant of Venice** with **Eric Porter** as both Barabas and Shylock.

**4.** Other Elizabethan/Jacobean dramatists began to be staged in Stratford. **Trevor Nunn's** first Stratford solo production was **The Revenger's Tragedy (1966)** (attributed to Tourneur). The production featured mostly new Company actors, many of whom have since become Associate Artists of the RSC. It also marked the beginning of Christopher Morley's design work with the Company and a return to flamboyance, although the production was done on a very tight budget: the *'costumes were made out of lining satin',* it became the season's biggest success.

**Alan Howard** (Lussurioso), **Ian Richardson** (Vendice).

*Photo: Gordon Goode*

**5. Trevor Nunn** followed with his production of **The Taming of the Shrew (1967)** in which **Michael Williams** (Petruchio) adopted a *'cowboy image — firing guns, riding barrels — a tongue-in-cheek, butch approach'.*

**Patrick Stewart** (Grumio), **Michael Williams** (Petruchio), **Janet Suzman** (Katharina)

*Photo: Tom Holte*

**6. As You Like It (1967)** was **David Jones'** first Stratford production.

**Roy Kinnear** (Touchstone), **Terrence Hardiman** (Corin).

**7. Peter Hall's** final production with the RSC was **Macbeth (1967)** with **Paul Scofield** and **Vivien Merchant** as the Macbeths.

*Photo: Reg Wilson*

**8. The Relapse (1967)** by Vanbrugh opened at the Aldwych the night after Macbeth opened in Stratford.

**Donald Sinden** (Lord Foppington).

*Photos 6 and 8: Douglas Jeffery*

6

1

8

2

## WORLD THEATRE SEASON

The Aldwych Theatre had become by this time, a *'showcase for international theatre',* jointly promoted, by **Peter Hall** and

**1. Peter Daubeny.**

The **World Theatre Seasons** (from 1964 to 1975), featured productions of 43 companies from 19 countries. These included:

**2. Kathakali Drama Company,** India. (1972).

**3.** One of the first productions was **Moscow Art Theatre: Dead Souls (1964)** by Gogol, dramatized by Mikhail Bulgakov.

*Photos 3, 4 and 5: over page*

The same year, the Aldwych welcomed the **Comédie Française:** *Un Fil a la Patte* (1964) by Feydeau, directed by Jacques Charon.

**4. Greek Art Theatre: The Birds (1964/5/7)** by Aristophanes, directed by **Karolos Koun.**

This was followed by the **Polish Contemporary Theatre:** *What a Lovely Dream* and *Let's Have Fun* (1964) by Slawomir Mrozek; **Theatre De France:** *Andromaque* (1965) by Racine, directed by Jean-Louis Barrault.

**5. Habimah National Theatre,** Israel: **The Dybbuk (1965)** by Salomon Anski.

Productions ranged from the **Actors' Studio Theatre,** USA: *Blues for Mister Charlie* (1965) by James Baldwin, directed by Burgess Meredith; to the **Czech National Theatre:** *The Insect Play* (1966) by Capek; to the **Noh Theatre of Japan:** *Hagoromo* (1967) with Kenzo Matsumoto.

91

**6. Bremen Theatre: Spring Awakening (1967)** by Wedekind, directed by **Peter Zadek.**

The following years saw a series of outstanding productions from the **Piccolo Theatre of Milan:** *The Servant of Two Masters* **(1967)** by Goldoni, directed by Giorgio Strehler; **Royal Dramatic Theatre,** Sweden: *Hedda Gabler* **(1968)** by Ibsen, directed by Ingmar Bergman; **Abbey Theatre,** Eire: *The Shaughraun* **(1968)** by Boucicault; **Theatre Behind the Gate,** Prague: *The Three Sisters* **(1969)** by Chekhov, directed by Otomar Krejca; **Anna Magnani's Company,** Italy: *La Lupa* **(1969)** by Vega, directed by Franco Zeffirelli; **Natal Theatre Workshop Zulu Company,** South Africa: *Umabatha* **(1973)** by Welcome Msomi, directed by Pieter Scholtz; **Eduardo De Filippo Company,** Italy: *Napoli Milionaria* **(1972)** by De Filippo, directed by and starring Eduardo De Filippo; **Nuria Espert Company,** Spain: *Yerma* **(1973)** by Lorca, directed by Victor Garcia with Nuria Espert; **Cracow Stary Theatre,** Poland: *The Possessed* **(1972/3)** by Dostoyevsky, directed by Andrzej Wajda.

*Photos: Morris Newcombe.*

By 1968, **Peter Hall** had moved the Company into regional and foreign tours, television and film productions, and non-Shakespearian and foreign drama. When **Trevor Nunn** took over, at 28 the youngest ever Artistic Director of the Company, Hall commented *'I have been in the hot seat for nine years and that is long enough'.*

92

3

4

5

6

# 7

## New Spaces
## New Themes
## 1968-1979

**1.** In 1968, **Trevor Nunn** inherited a unique theatrical empire. He restructured its management and established a team to give an administrative as well as artistic framework to the Company, initially with three directors: **John Barton, Terry Hands** and **David Jones.** Jones later became administrator and artistic director of the Aldwych Theatre.

*Photo: Zoë Dominic*

## THE TRANSITION

During Peter Hall's final year, Nunn continued to direct notable productions in Stratford, all designed by Christopher Morley:

**2. King Lear (1968)** featured **Eric Porter** as Lear and **Michael Williams** as the Fool. Michael Williams saw the Fool as *'something of a monkey, clinging to Lear. I went to the Zoo to study the monkeys. There I saw Alec McCowen who revealed that he had modelled his Fool on a red monkey . . . I chose a different one.'*

**Patrick Stewart** (Cornwall), **Susan Fleetwood** (Regan), **Eric Porter** (King Lear), **Sheila Allen** (Goneril), **Michael Williams** (Fool), **Diane Fletcher** (Cordelia), **Terrence Hardiman** (Albany).

*Photo: Reg Wilson*

**3. Much Ado About Nothing (1968)** with **Alan Howard** (Benedick) and **Janet Suzman** (Beatrice).

*Photo: Zoë Dominic*

94

**5**

**2**

**1**

**4. Terry Hands** made his Stratford debut as director with **The Merry Wives of Windsor (1968).**

**Jeffery Dench** (Page), **Sydney Bromley** (Shallow).

*Photo: Nobby Clark*

**5. John Barton's Troilus and Cressida (1968)** was an athletic production. **Michael Williams** (Troilus) recalls: *'a lot of sword fighting, and with John Barton as fight director one became proficient in the art of fighting!'*

**Alan Howard** (Achilles).

*Photo: Reg Wilson*

Nunn consolidated and rationalised the innovations of his predecessor. He set up two, smaller, acting companies: one in Stratford and the other in London. Productions transferred from Stratford to London at the end of the season, while the London company rehearsed for the next Stratford season.

## LONDON

The London Company continued to present classical revivals and new plays at the Aldwych Theatre, including:

**1. Landscape** and **Silence (1969),** a double bill by Harold Pinter, directed by **Peter Hall.**

**David Waller** (Duff), **Peggy Ashcroft** (Beth) in **Landscape.**

*Photo: Zoë Dominic*

**2. Tiny Alice (1970)** by Edward Albee, directed by **Robin Phillips.**

**Ray McAnally** (Lawyer), **Richard Pearson** (Cardinal), **David Warner** (Julian), **Irene Worth** (Miss Alice).

*Photo: Zoë Dominic*

**3. Old Times (1971)** by Harold Pinter, directed by **Peter Hall.**

**Dorothy Tutin** (Kate), **Colin Blakely** (Deeley), **Vivien Merchant** (Anna).

*Photo: Zoë Dominic*

**4. The Balcony (1971/2)** by Jean Genet, directed by **Terry Hands.**

**T.P. McKenna** (Bishop), **Clement McCallin** (Judge), **Philip Locke** (General), **Brenda Bruce** (Queen/Irma), **Barry Stanton** (Chief of Police, *seated*).

*Photo: Douglas Jeffery*

**5. The Man of Mode (1971)** by Etherege was directed by **Terry Hands.**

**Alan Howard** (Dorimant), **Brenda Bruce** (Lady Townley), **Frances de la Tour** (Bellinda), **Isla Blair** (Emilia), **Julian Glover** (Medley).

*Photo: Reg Wilson*

**6. Murder In The Cathedral (1972)** by T.S. Eliot, was directed by **Terry Hands.**

**Anthony Pedley** (2nd Tempter/Knight), **Bernard Lloyd** (1st Tempter/Knight), **Tony Church** (3rd Tempter/Knight), **Nickolas Grace** (2nd Priest), **Denis Holmes** (1st Priest), **Morgan Sheppard** (3rd Priest), **Richard Pasco** (Becket).

*Photo: John Haynes*

**7. Sherlock Holmes (1974)** by Conan Doyle/Gillette, directed by **Frank Dunlop.**

**John Wood** (Sherlock Holmes), **Tim Pigott-Smith** (Dr Watson).

*Photo: Reg Wilson*

**8. The Bewitched (1974)** by Peter Barnes, directed by **Terry Hands.**

**Mark Dignam** (Valladar), **Alan Howard** (Carlos II), **Trevor Peacock** (Father Motilla), **Joe Melia** (Father Froylan).
*Photo: Nobby Clark*

**9. Dr Faustus (1974)** by Christopher Marlowe, directed by **John Barton.**

**Ian McKellen** (Faustus).
*Photo: Donald Cooper*

**10. Hedda Gabler (1975)** by Henrik Ibsen was adapted and directed by **Trevor Nunn.**
**Glenda Jackson** (Hedda), **Jennie Linden** (Mrs Elvsted).
*Photo: Philip Sayer*

**11. The Iceman Cometh (1976)** by Eugene O'Neill, directed by **Howard Davies.**

**Patrick Stewart** (Larry Slade), **Bob Hoskins** (Rocky).
*Photo: Laurence Burns*

**12. Old World (1976)** by Aleksei Arbuzov, directed by **Terry Hands.**

**Anthony Quayle** (Rodion). **Peggy Ashcroft** (Lidya),
*Photo: Zoë Dominic*

**13. Pillars of The Community (1977)** by Henrik Ibsen, directed by **John Barton.**

**Ian McKellen** (Karsten Bernick), **Paola Dionisotti** (Martha Bernick), **Eliza Ward** (Betty Bernick), **Paul Brooke** (Hilmar Tönnesen), **Tony Church** (Rörlund), **Denyse Alexander** (Mrs Holt), **Judi Dench** (Lona Hessel).
*Photo: Sophie Baker*

# THEATREGOROUND

Theatregoround (TGR) was started in 1965 during **Peter Hall's** period as Artistic Director of the RSC and flourished during the early years after **Trevor Nunn** took over, finally succumbing to lack of funding in the early Seventies. Founded by **Michael Kustow**, **John Barton** and **Terry Hands** — who became TGR's first Artistic Director — Theatregoround's work spanned small-scale touring, festivals, courses for teachers, Aldwych 'flare-ups' (which included poetry readings and demonstrations) as well as plays, and a notable 1970 season at The Round House including **Peter Brook's A Midsummer Night's Dream**, **Trevor Nunn's Hamlet** and **Terry Hand's Richard III** staged without set or costume. **Gareth Morgan** took over as Artistic Director in 1968 and other directors involved in TGR included **Buzz Goodbody**, **Clifford Williams** and **Mike Leigh**. Thereafter, small-auditorium work and later small-scale tours owed much to the experience of TGR.

**When Thou Art King (1970)** was a TGR adaptation by **John Barton** of Shakespeare's **Henry IV** plays and **Henry V**, directed by **Barton** and **Gareth Morgan**. It was in three parts: **The Battle of Shrewsbury**, **The Rejection of Falstaff** and **The Battle of Agincourt**.

**1. The Rejection of Falstaff** (from **Henry IV Part 2**). **Anne Dyson** (Mistress Quickly), **Don Henderson** (Bardolph), **Jeffery Dench** (Pistol), **Brewster Mason** (Falstaff), **Gordon Reid** (Francis).

*Photo: Douglas Jeffery*

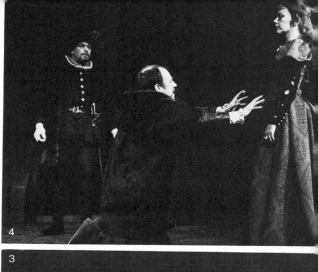

2. **Dr. Faustus (1970)** by Christopher Marlowe, directed by **Gareth Morgan.**

**David Waller** (Faustus), **Clement McCallin** (Pope Adrian), **Ralph Cotterill** (Bruno the Anti-Pope, *crouching*), **Alan Howard** (Mephistophiles).
*Photo: Douglas Jeffery*

3. **King John (1970)** directed by **Buzz Goodbody** was, for **Norman Rodway,** *'a marvellous production . . . like a strip cartoon . . . very effective'.*

**Patrick Stewart** (King John), **Peter Needham** (Philip of France), **Michael McGovern** (Citizen of Angiers, *above*).
*Photo: Donald Cooper*

4. **Arden of Faversham (1970)** by an unknown author, directed by **Buzz Goodbody.**

**Richard Mayes** (Franklin), **Emrys James** (Arden), **Dorothy Tutin** (Alice).

*Photo: Reg Wilson*

### THE PLACE

In 1971, the company took a short lease on **The Place,** in London, where a number of new plays were presented, including:

1. **Occupations (1971)** by Trevor Griffiths, directed by **Buzz Goodbody.**

**Ben Kingsley** (Gramsci), **Patrick Stewart** (Kabak).
*Photo: J. Styles*

2. **Cries From Casement As His Bones Are Brought To Dublin (1973)** by David Rudkin, directed by **Terry Hands.**

**Colin Blakely** (Casement), **Malcolm Kaye, Margaret Whiting, Nicholas Selby, Rosemary McHale, Geoffrey Hutchings.** *Photo: Nobby Clark*

3. *(see over page)*

**3. Section Nine (1973)** by Philip Magdalany, directed by **Charles Marowitz.**

**Patrick Godfrey** (Dr Swayze), **Harry Towb** (Adrian Mackenzie), **Peter Schofield** (Man), **Geoffrey Hutchings** (Jasper 906), **Joe Melia** (Attendant), **Judy Geeson** (Vivien 532), **Norman Rossington** (General Muster) **David Waller** (Senator Caldwell), **Margaret Whiting** (Winifred 601), **Stephen Moore** (Fenwick 747), **Gareth Hunt** (Marlon 845).

*Photo: Donald Cooper*

## THEMES

**1.** During the Seventies, **David Jones** initiated a revival of interest in Russian dramatists particularly Gorky, with four Gorky/Jones productions:
*Photo: John Haynes*

**2. Enemies (1971)** was **David Jones'** first Gorky production at the Aldwych Theatre.

**Patrick Stewart** (Mikhail), **Alan Howard** (Skrobotov), **Brenda Bruce** (Paulina), **Lila Kaye** (Agrafena), **Philip Locke** (Zakhar Bardin), **John Wood** (Yakov).

*Photo: Reg Wilson*

**3. The Lower Depths (1972).**

**Tony Church** (Kostylyob) **Gordon Gostelow** (Luka)

**4. Summerfolk (1974).**

**Sebastian Shaw** (Dvoetochie) **Mike Gwilym** (Vlass) **Tony Church** (Suslov)
*Photos: Donald Cooper*

**5. The Zykovs (1976).**

**Mia Farrow** (Pavla), **Paul Rogers** (Antipa Ivanich Zykov).
*Photo: John Haynes*

7

8

6

In Stratford, **Trevor Nunn** and **Terry Hands** moved from the historical focus of the Sixties to a thematic approach, directing Shakespeare's late plays in a vast chamber setting with a predominantly young company, using a single-set design by Christopher Morley, known as 'the white box'.

**6. The Winter's Tale (1969)**, directed by **Trevor Nunn**, was set in the 'white box'. Another device in this season's productions was the use of actors doubling in key roles. **Judi Dench** played both Hermione and Perdita. This required precision timing at the end of the play, when she had to change from Perdita seeing Hermione's statue into Hermione herself, seen in a glass box.

**Judi Dench** (Hermione).
**Jeremy Richardson** (Mamillius),
**Barrie Ingham** (Leontes),
**Richard Pasco** (Polixenes),
                    *Photo: Reg Wilson*

**7. Pericles (1969)**, directed by **Terry Hands** featured **Susan Fleetwood** doubling as Thaisa and Marina.

**Ian Richardson** (Pericles).
                    *Photo: Reg Wilson*

**8. Henry VIII (1969)**, directed by **Trevor Nunn**.

**Michael Gambon** (Surrey), **Donald Sinden** (King), **Nicholas Selby** (Lord Chamberlain), **Dennis Holmes** (Suffolk).
                    *Photo: Zoë Dominic*

In 1972, **Trevor Nunn** directed all four of Shakespeare's Roman plays: **"The Romans"**. For these productions the theatre boasted a new stage hydraulics system as well as a remodelled auditorium.

**1. Coriolanus (1972),** with **Ian Hogg** in the title role. **Nicol Williamson** took over for the transfer to the Aldwych.

**Patrick Stewart** (Tullus Aufidius, *centre*).

**2. Julius Caesar (1972).**

*Centre:* **Mark Dignam** (Caesar),**John Wood** (Brutus).

**3. Antony and Cleopatra (1972).**

**Janet Suzman** (Cleopatra), **Richard Johnson** (Antony), **Patrick Stewart** (Enobarbus).

**4. Titus Andronicus (1972).**

**Ian Hogg** (Lucius), **Janet Suzman** (Lavinia), **Colin Blakely** (Titus), **Mark Dignam** (Marcus).

*Photos: Reg Wilson*

A financial crisis in 1974 proved a turning point for the Company. **Terry Hands** devoted himself to Stratford's RST for its 1975 season, with a programme of **Henry V** and **Henry IV parts 1 and 2,** together with a revival of **The Merry Wives of Windsor,** using just 25 actors (the 1964 cycle had used nearly 50). The 1977 season included a revival of **Henry V,** together with the RSC's first unabridged **Henry VI** trilogy. The cycle was also notable for Farrah's highly symbolic designs which conveyed *'both intimacy and the breadth of action on the battlefield'.*

102

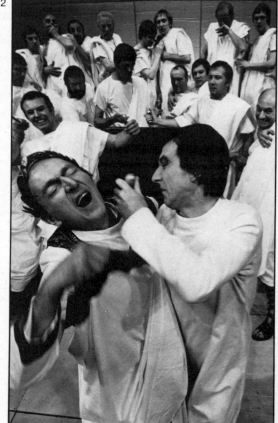

**Alan Howard** was to play four Shakespearian kings over the next five years under **Terry Hands'** direction and added **Coriolanus** to his repertoire at the end of the 1977 season.

**5.Henry V** *(photograph of Aldwych transfer, 1976).*

**Oliver Ford-Davies** (Montjoy), **Stephen Jenn** (Gloucester), **Alan Howard** (Henry V), **Richard Moore** (Pistol), **Jeffery Dench** (Gower), **Trevor Peacock** (Fluellen).
*Photo: Robert Pascall*

**6. Henry IV, Part 2 (1975).**

**Trevor Peacock** (Silence), **Brewster Mason** (Falstaff), **Ben Wellstood** (Falstaff's Page), **Tim Wylton** (Bardolph), **Sydney Bromley** (Shallow), **Philip Brack** (Davy).
*Photo: Donald Cooper*

**7. Henry VI, Part 2 (1977).**

**Helen Mirren** (Queen Margaret), **Alan Howard** (Henry VI).
*Photo: Joe Cocks*

**8. Henry VI, Part 3 (1977).**

**Alan Howard** (Henry VI), **Anton Lesser** (Gloucester).
*Photo: Nobby Clark*

These epics became a focal point of the RSC's work during the Seventies. **Oliver Ford-Davies** recalls the *'particular atmosphere when three plays were performed in one day, usually on a Saturday starting at 10.30am and ending at 11.00pm.'*

## CONTINUED EXPANSION

**1.** A new approach to the use of space and light was hallmarked by a spectacular beginning to the Seventies: **Peter Brook's** production of **A Midsummer Night's Dream (1970).** Designed by Sally Jacobs, it involved an energetic display of Chinese acrobatics and magic. Even the sounds were unconventional, composed by Richard Peaslee. Critical approval sent the production from Stratford to Broadway, New York and back to London, and, between August 1972-August 1973, on a worldwide tour including Japan and Australia.

**Alan Howard** (Oberon), **Sara Kestelman** (Titania), **John Kane** (Puck).

*Photo Reg Wilson*

Titania's bower of ostrich feathers could be lowered and raised as required.

Other notable Stratford productions during this period included:

**2. Twelfth Night (1969),** a 'Chekhovian' production designed by Christopher Morley and directed by **John Barton.**

**Lisa Harrow** (Olivia), **Judi Dench** (Viola), **Donald Sinden** (Malvolio).

*Photo: Zoë Dominic*

**3. Othello (1971),** directed by **John Barton** and set in 19th-century barracks.

**Matthew Robertson** (First Officer), **Emrys James** (Iago), **Miles Anderson** (Soldier), **David Calder** (Cassio).

*Photo: Philip Sayer*

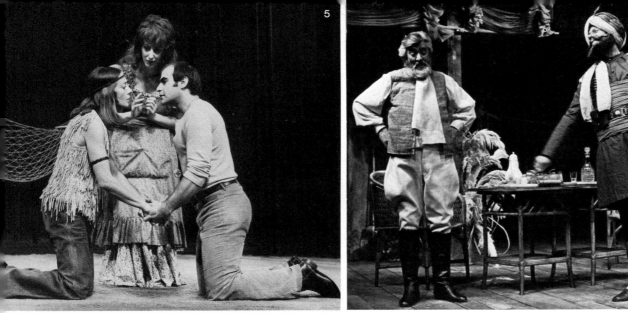

5

6

7

8

**4. Richard II (1973)** directed by **John Barton**. Richard Pasco and Ian Richardson alternated the roles of Bolingbroke and the King.

**Richard Pasco** (Richard II), **Ian Richardson** (Bolingbroke).
*Photo: Donald Cooper*

**5. As You Like It (1973)** directed by **Buzz Goodbody**.

**David Suchet** (understudying **Bernard Lloyd** as Orlando) was given three days to learn and rehearse the role before the first preview when Lloyd could not appear. In addition, **Eileen Atkins** (Rosalind) had sprained her ankle, so that, *'I had to improvise a whole dance by myself'*. During his first Stratford season, Suchet had played all his understudy roles.

**Eileen Atkins** (Rosalind), **Maureen Lipman** (Celia), **David Suchet** (Orlando).
*Photo: Zoë Dominic*

**6. Much Ado About Nothing (1976)** in a colonial Indian setting directed by **John Barton**.

**Ivan Beavis** (Leonato), **John Woodvine** (Dogberry), **Norman Tyrrell** (Verges).
*Photo: Nobby Clark*

**7. King Lear (1976),** directed by **Trevor Nunn** and designed by John Napier on the 1976 timber set.

**Michael Williams** (Fool), **Donald Sinden** (Lear).
*Photo: Donald Cooper*

**8. Coriolanus (1977),** directed by **Terry Hands** with designs by Farrah. The production clearly illustrated the private and public dilemma of its protagonist. Much praised, it toured Europe in 1979.

**Alan Howard** (Coriolanus).
*Photo: Reg Wilson*

**9. Romeo and Juliet (1976)**, directed by **Trevor Nunn**, with **Ian McKellen** and **Francesca Annis** in the title-roles.

*Photo: Nobby Clark*

**10. A Midsummer Night's Dream (1977)**, directed by **John Barton** with **Gillian Lynne**, designed by John Napier.

**Marjorie Bland** (Titania), **Patrick Stewart** (Oberon).

*Photo: Anthony Crickmay*

**11. Measure for Measure (1978)**, marked **Barry Kyle's** directorial debut at the RST. **Sinead Cusack** replaced **Paola Dionisetti** when the play transferred to the Aldwych.

**Michael Pennington** (The Duke), **Sinead Cusack** (Isabella).

**12. Love's Labour's Lost (1978)**, directed by **John Barton**, designed by Ralph Koltai.

**Ian Charleson** (Longaville), **Paul Whitworth** (Dumaine), **Michael Pennington** (Berowne), **Richard Griffiths** (Navarre).

*Photo: Donald Cooper*

13. In 1978, **Peter Brook** returned to direct **Antony and Cleopatra** with **Alan Howard** and **Glenda Jackson** in the title-roles.

*Photo: Reg Wilson*

14. **The Taming of The Shrew (1978)**, directed by **Michael Bogdanov**, designed by Chris Dyer.

**Jonathan Pryce** (Petruchio), **David Suchet** (Grumio), **David Lyon** (Hortensio).

*Photo: Laurence Burns*

The production opened with **Jonathan Pryce** dressed as a drunken tramp (Christopher Sly) mounting the stage from the auditorium and tearing down the stage scenery, before turning into Petruchio. This unusual beginning often prompted members of the audience to ask theatre staff to call for the police. Another leapt on to the stage, and proceeded to grab Jonathan Pryce by the throat *'...He was eventually led off in a state of complete confusion.'*

15. **The Merry Wives of Windsor (1979)**, directed by **Trevor Nunn** and **John Caird**, designed by John Napier.

**Ben Kingsley** (Ford), **John Woodvine** (Falstaff).

*Photo: Donald Cooper*

16. **Twelfth Night (1979)**, directed by **Terry Hands**, designed by John Napier.

**Kate Nicholls** (Olivia), **Jane Downs** (Maria), **John Woodvine** (Malvolio).

*Photo: Reg Wilson*

# THE OTHER PLACE

**1.** Stratford did not acquire its 'official' studio theatre, The Other Place (TOP) until 1974. But its origins went back much further. The tin shack that became The Other Place was a rehearsal space and store by the early Seventies, but had earlier been used by Michel Saint-Denis as an experimental acting studio.

*All TOP photos by Joe Cocks unless otherwise credited.*

**2. Buzz Goodbody**, the RSC's first woman director, became the first artistic director of The Other Place. She had originally joined the RSC in 1967 as John Barton's personal assistant and was for several years Assistant Director to Terry Hands. **Cicely Berry** (the Company's head of Voice) recalls her *'deep respect for the actors. She allowed them to find themselves on the stage, so that they knew they belonged.'*

*Photo: Topix*

**3. Lear (1974)**, a version of Shakespeare's play, directed by **Buzz Goodbody** was the opening production in the first official The Other Place season.

**Tony Church** (Lear), **David Suchet** (Fool).

**4. Hamlet (1975)** under **Buzz Goodbody's** direction was in modern dress.

**Mikel Lambert** (Gertrude), **Ben Kingsley** (Hamlet).

Ben Kingsley says *'It was while performing in Buzz Goodbody's production of* Hamlet *that I really appreciated the implications of that famous line "to hold, as 'twere, the mirror up to nature"... Since the advent of The Other Place, we have*

learned to brave a much closer level of scrutiny from our audience, moving from "us and them" to "you and I".'

**5. Man is Man (1975)** by Brecht directed by **Howard Davies**, designed by Chris Dyer.

**Sidney Livingstone** (Jesse Mahoney), **Ben Kingsley** (Mr Wang), **Bob Peck** (Uriah Shelley), **Philip Dunbar** (Polly Baker), **Gareth Armstrong** (Jeriah Jip).

**6. Destiny (1976),** the *'finest political play of the decade,'* by David Edgar. The study of the evolution of a National Front-style party, directed by **Ron Daniels**, later transferred successfully to the Aldwych Theatre's larger stage.

**Michael Pennington** (Major Rolfe), **Ian McDiarmid** (Turner), **Marc Zuber** (Gurjeet Singh Khera), **David Lyon** (Colonel Chandler).

**7. Schweyk in the Second World War (1976)** by Bertolt Brecht, directed by **Howard Davies.**

**Michael Williams** (Schweyk), **Paul Brooke** (Baloun). Williams gave Schweyk a 'music-hall characterisation.'

**8. John Woodvine** (Banquo), **Ian McKellen** (Macbeth), with the Weird Sisters.

**Macbeth (1976)** was **Trevor Nunn's** third production of this play. He stripped it down to essentials: the actors were on view even when they took no part in the action and there was no interval. Ian McKellen recalls, *'John Napier (the designer) gave us a painted circle as a stage . . .our only furniture was beer crates. All the costumes were second-hand junk.*

*It all cost about £250.'* An actor participated in the action only if he stepped inside the circle. Highly stylised, it became a hallucinatory experience for the audience. The production also played at the RST, the Warehouse, transferred to the Young Vic for two months, and in 1978 was filmed by Thames Television.

In 1977, **Ron Daniels** became Artistic Director of TOP.

**9. The Sons of Light (1977)** by David Rudkin, directed by **Ron Daniels.**

**Charlotte Cornwell** (Child Manatond), **Peter McEnery** (Yescanab).

**10. The Alchemist (1977)** by Ben Jonson, directed by **Trevor Nunn,** was played at an incredible farce-like pace.

**John Woodvine** (Subtle), **Susan Dury** (Doll Common), **Ian McKellen** (Face).

**11. The Merchant of Venice (1978),** directed by **John Barton.**

**Patrick Stewart** (Shylock), **Avril Carson** (Jessica).

**12. Pericles (1979)** directed by **Ron Daniels.**

**Peter McEnery** (Pericles), **Suzanne Bertish** (Dionyza), **Nigel Terry** (Cleon).

**13. Captain Swing (1979)** by Peter Whelan, directed by **Bill Alexander.**

**Zoë Wanamaker** (Gemma Beech), **Malcolm Storry** (Farquarson), **Hilton McRae** (Daniel).

*Photo: Donald Cooper*

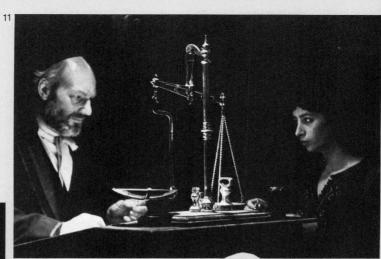

**14. Baal (1979)** by Brecht in a translation by Peter Tegel, directed by **David Jones.**

**Nigel Terry** (Ekart), **Ben Kingsley** (Baal).

**15. The Suicide (1979)** by Nikolai Erdman, directed by **Ron Daniels,** transferred to the Aldwych.

**Roger Rees** (Semyon, *centre),* with **Emily Richard** (Cleopatra), **Peter Clough** (Egor), **Shirley King** (Raissa), **Timothy Kightley** (Kalabushkin), **Susan Tracy** (Maria), **Lila Kaye** (Serafima).

## THE WAREHOUSE

In 1977, the RSC acquired an equivalent small space theatre in London: The Warehouse, in Covent Garden. It had been a banana warehouse. Occasionally an actor appeared at both The Warehouse and the Aldwych on the same evening. **Griffith Jones** was Egeus in **A Midsummer Night's Dream** at the Aldwych Theatre and Duncan in **Macbeth** at the Warehouse. He played the first scene of *The Dream,* walked up the road to The Warehouse to play Duncan, was killed and walked back to the Aldwych, and appeared in the last scene of *The Dream.* The danger arose if the curtain at the Aldwych went up late. . .

**Howard Davies** became its Artistic Director and instigated a policy of doing new plays by contemporary British writers, such as:

**1. That Good Between Us (1977)** by Howard Barker, directed by **Barry Kyle.**

**Ian McDiarmid** (McPhee), **John Nettles** (Godber).

**2. Bandits (1977)** by CP Taylor, directed by **Howard Davies.**

**Bob Peck** (Ray Purvis).
*Photo: Chris Davies*

**3. Factory Birds (1977)** by James Robson, directed by **Bill Alexander.**

**Roger Rees** (Nazzer), **Rod Culbertson** (Tojo).
*Photos 1&3: George Xanthos*

**4. The Jail Diary of Albie Sachs (1978)** by David Edgar, directed by **Howard Davies.**

**Peter McEnery** (Albie Sachs), **Peter Clough** (Sergeant), **John Burgess** (Constable).
*Photo: Donald Cooper*

**5. The Bundle (1977)** by Edward Bond, specially written for the Warehouse and directed by **Howard Davies.**

**Margaret Ashcroft** (Ferryman's Wife), **Paul Moriarty** (Tiger), **Mike Gwilym** (Wang), **Bob Peck** (Ferryman).
*Photo: Chris Davies*

**6. Savage Amusement (1978)** by Peter Flannery, directed by **John Caird.**

**Iain Mitchell** (Stephen), **Jill Baker** (Hazel), **David Threlfall** (Fitz), **Charles Wegner** (Olly), **Lesley Manville** (Ali).
*Photo: Donald Cooper*

## OTHER DIRECTIONS

During 1977, the RSC made the first of its annual visits to Newcastle's Theatre Royal and Gulbenkian Studio between the end of the Stratford season (January) and the start of the Aldwych season in London.

1

2

4

3

5

6

7

8

In 1978, the RSC launched another venture: a small-scale tour led by the actor Ian McKellen, to 26 British towns and villages. It played town halls, corn exchanges and *'a battered 18th-century church'*.

**7. Three Sisters (1978)** by Chekhov, in a translation by Richard Cottrell, directed by **Trevor Nunn,** was an outstanding success. It was later seen at TOP and the Warehouse and on television.

**Emily Richard** (Irina), **Suzanne Bertish** (Masha), **Susan Tracy** (Natalya), **Bridget Turner** (Olga).
*Photo: Chris Davies*

Music has played a major part in all RSC productions: Guy Woolfenden, the Head of Music, joined as Assistant Music Director in 1962. In the Seventies, productions used music and choreography in a new way.

**8. The Comedy of Errors (1976),** directed by **Trevor Nunn,** was a musical version, as had been Komisarjevsky's in the 1930s, which made great demands on the actors' athletic skills. It was filmed by Thames Television and was voted the best musical of the year by the Society of West End Theatre.

*(Standing)* **Nickolas Grace** (Dromio of Ephesus), **Mike Gwilym** (Antipholus of Ephesus).

**Nickolas Grace** recalls the *'tricky acrobatics'* devised by the choreographer Gillian Lynne. One night when he *'leapt back onstage, an enthusiastic spectator in the front row grabbed my arm and threw me off balance . . . he said "you were wonderful, wonderful — just like Jimmy Saville" . . . Jim didn't fix this* *one! The spectator went home happy. The actor went to hospital with a snapped Achilles tendon.'*

**1. Once In A Lifetime (1979)** by Hart and Kaufman. Directed by **Trevor Nunn** with designs by John Napier and intricate choreography by Gillian Lynne.

**Paul Brooke** (Kammerling), **David Suchet** (Glogauer), **Tonia Fuller** (Susan Walker), **Richard Griffiths** (George Lewis), **Peter McEnery** (Jerry Hyland), **Zoë Wanamaker** (May Daniels).

*Photos: Donald Cooper*

West End transfers included:

**2. After Haggerty (1970)** by David Mercer, directed by **David Jones,** was the first RSC play to transfer to the West End.

**Billie Whitelaw** (Claire), **Leslie Sands** (Mr Link) **Frank Finlay** (Bernard)

*Photo: Zoë Dominic*

**3. London Assurance (1970)** by Dion Boucicault, directed by **Ronald Eyre.**

**Donald Sinden** (Sir William Courtly).

*Photo: Reg Wilson*

**4. Travesties (1974)** by Tom Stoppard, directed by **Peter Wood.**

**Maria Aitken** (Gwendolen), **John Hurt** (Tristan Tzara), **John Bott** (Bennett), **Tom Bell** (James Joyce), **Beth Morris** (Cecily), **John Wood** (Henry Carr).

*Photo: Sophie Baker*

**5. Too True To Be Good (1975)** by Bernard Shaw, directed by **Clifford Williams.**

**Judi Dench** (The Countess/ Nurse Sweetie Simpkins), **Ian McKellen** (Aubrey Bagot/ The Burglar), **Anna Calder Marshall** (Miss Mopply/The Patient).

*Photo: Zoë Dominic*

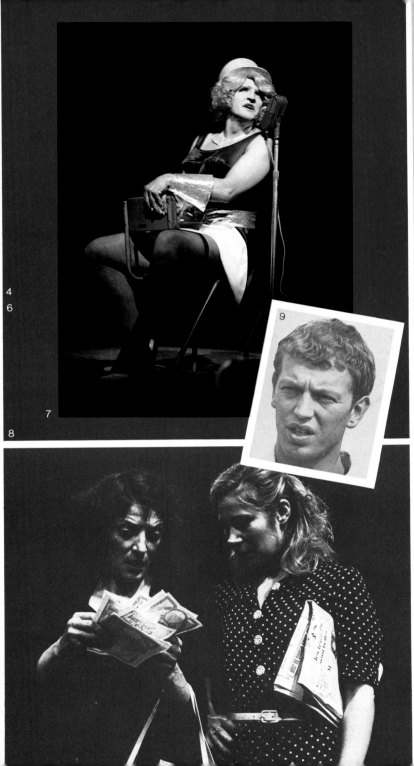

**6. Wild Oats (1976)** by John O'Keeffe, directed by **Clifford Williams.**

**Norman Rodway** (Sir George Thunder), **Alan Howard** (Jack Rover).

*Photo: Reg Wilson*

The rediscovery of this play (last performed at Stratford by Compton's Company in 1882), about an actor's mistaken identity, was an overwhelming (and unexpected) success at the Aldwych Theatre, was transferred to Stratford in the winter season and finally to the Piccadilly Theatre in London for a successful commercial run.

**7.** Peter Nichols' **Privates on Parade (1977),** directed by **Michael Blakemore.** A musical that enjoyed a West End transfer and was filmed, it dealt with Nichols' recollections of ENSA in 1940s Malaya.

**Dennis Quilley** (Acting Captain Terri Denis).

*Photo: Reg Wilson*

### BROADWAY

**8. Piaf (1979)** by Pam Gems, directed by **Howard Davies,** began its life at The Other Place, transferred to The Warehouse, the West End and then Broadway.

**Zoë Wanamaker** (Toine) recalls how she and **Jane Lapotaire** (Piaf) improvised what their characters would do when they got some money, how they could 'abuse it': *'we stuck it up our noses, in our ears, in our knickers, in our bras'.*

**9.** In 1978 **Terry Hands** joined **Trevor Nunn** as joint Artistic Director.

During the 1979 season, the RSC staged a total of 33 plays with a company of 175 actors.

## EPILOGUE

The Company in Stratford-upon-Avon entered the Eighties and so began its second century. Major RST productions in the next few years included:

**1. Richard II** and **Richard III (1980),** directed by **Terry Hands,** designed by Farrah, and with **Alan Howard** in the title-roles, completed the full cycle of Shakespeare's history plays initiated in 1975.

**Alan Howard** (Richard II), **David Suchet** (Bolingbroke).

**Sinead Cusack** (Lady Anne), **Alan Howard** (Richard III).

*Photos: Nobby Clark*

**2. All's Well That Ends Well (1981),** directed by **Trevor Nunn,** played in Stratford, Newcastle, London and then on Broadway.

*Foreground:* **Robert Eddison** (Lafeu), **Stephen Moore** (Parolles), **Cheryl Campbell** (Diana), **John Franklyn-Robbins** (King of France), **Harriet Walter** (Helena), **Mike Gwilym** (Bertram), **Peter Land** (Dumaine), **Peggy Ashcroft** (Countess of Rossillion).

**3. King Lear (1982)** was **Adrian Noble's** directorial debut at the RST.

**Antony Sher** (Fool).
**Michael Gambon** (Lear),

*All photographs by Donald Cooper unless otherwise credited.*

116

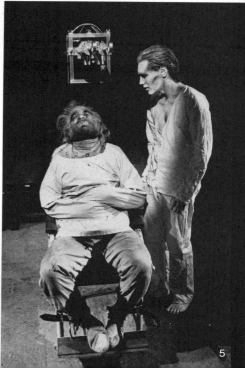

6

7

8

4

**4. Much Ado About Nothing (1982)** directed by **Terry Hands** and designed by Ralph Koltai. In addition to playing at Stratford, Newcastle and London, it toured Europe and was presented together with *Cyrano de Bergerac*, at the Los Angeles Olympic Arts Festival (1984), on Broadway and in Washington.

**Derek Jacobi** (Benedick), **Sinead Cusack** (Beatrice).

Meanwhile, The Other Place achieved further success with contemporary works and classics including:

**5. Lear (1982)** by Edward Bond, directed by **Barry Kyle** and designed by Kit Surrey (it played opposite *King Lear*). The production toured Europe with *Much Ado About Nothing*.

**Bob Peck** (Lear), **Mark Rylance** (Gravedigger's Boy).

**6. A Doll's House (1981)** by Ibsen in a translation by Michael Meyer, directed by **Adrian Noble.**

**Cheryl Campbell** (Nora), **Stephen Moore** (Torvald).
                    *Photo: Nobby Clark*

**7. Molière (1982)** by Bulgakov in a new version by Dusty Hughes, directed by **Bill Alexander** and designed by Ralph Koltai. The production was also filmed for television.

**Antony Sher** (Moliere), **David Troughton** (Bouton).
                    *Photo: Mark Williamson*

**8. Peer Gynt (1982)** by Ibsen in a translation by David Rudkin, directed by **Ron Daniels** and designed by Chris Dyer.

**Derek Jacobi** (Peer Gynt).

**1. The Dillen (1983)** was adapted by Ron Hutchinson from the true story of George Hewins (a Stratford working man), by Angela Hewins. The production, directed by **Barry Kyle** and designed by Chris Dyer, opened each performance at TOP but then took audience and performers (who included many local people) into the streets and fields of Stratford.

*On bus steps:* **Ron Cook** (George "Cookie" Hewins), **Dickie Arnold** (Old George), **Paul Basson** (Young George).

The RSC's final years at the Aldwych also witnessed some outstanding productions including:

**The Greeks (1980),** a ten-play cycle, performed over three nights ("The War", "The Murders", "The Gods"), adapted from the works of Euripedes, Homer, Aeschylus and Sophocles by John Barton and Kenneth Cavander. It was directed by **John Barton** and designed by John Napier.

**2. The War (The Trojan Women).**

*(foreground)* **Eliza Ward** (Hecuba), **Hugo Simpson** (Astyanax), **Billie Whitelaw** (Andromache).

**3. The Murders (Agamemnon).**

**Janet Suzman** (Clytemnestra), **John Shrapnel** (Agamemnon).
*Photo: Reg Wilson*

**4. The Life and Adventures of Nicholas Nickleby (1980)** was one of the high points of the Company's ensemble playing over the years. Adapted from the Dickens novel by David Edgar, it was directed by **Trevor Nunn** and **John Caird** and designed by John Napier and played three separate

seasons at the Aldwych before transferring to Broadway. It was also filmed for television.

**Roger Rees** (Nicholas Nickleby), **David Threlfall** (Smike) and the company.

Successful productions at The Warehouse led to West End transfers:

**5. Educating Rita (1980)** by Willy Russell, directed by **Mike Ockrent.** The play on transferring to the West End, became one of the longest-running shows in the Piccadilly Theatre's history. It subsequently toured the country and was then the basis of a film in which **Julie Walters** also starred, opposite **Michael Caine.**

**Mark Kingston** (Frank), **Julie Walters** (Rita).

*Photo: John Haynes*

**6. Good (1981)** was C.P. Taylor's last play. Directed by **Howard Davies,** it transferred to the Aldwych and then to Broadway.

**Nicholas Woodeson** (Bouller), **Felicity Dean** (Anne), **Pip Miller** (Freddie), **Penelope Beaumont** (Nurse), **Alan Howard** (Halder), **Nigel Hess** (Musician), **Chris Hunter** (Hitler), **Joe Melia** (Maurice).

*Photo: Alastair Muir*

**7.** In 1982, the RSC transferred its London base to the Barbican Centre.

**8.** The Barbican Theatre opened with **Henry IV Parts 1** and **2 (1982)** directed by **Trevor Nunn** and designed by John Napier — the same plays which had opened the Shakespeare Memorial Theatre in 1932.

**Timothy Dalton** (Hotspur), **Gerard Murphy** (Hal).

**9.** *(see over page)*

119

**9. Our Friends in The North (1982)** by Peter Flannery, directed by **John Caird,** was the first production in The Pit

**David Whitaker** (Geordie), **Joseph Marcell** (Joseph).

The Barbican has confirmed the Royal Shakespeare Company's innovative tradition with:

**1. Poppy (1982)** by Peter Nichols and Monty Norman, directed by **Terry Hands.** It subsequently transferred to the West End.

*Centre:* **Julia Hills** (Sally Forth), **Geraldine Gardner** (Dick Whittington), **Geoffrey Hutchings** (Lady Dodo).

**2. Peter Pan (1982)** by J.M. Barrie, directed by **Trevor Nunn** and **John Caird** and designed by John Napier, was a major success repeated at Christmas 1983 and 1984.

**Jane Carr** (Wendy), **Miles Anderson** (Peter).

*Photo: Sophie Baker*

**3. Maydays (1983)** by David Edgar, directed by **Ron Daniels.**

**Bob Peck** (Lermontov), **Ken Bones** (Paloczi), **Antony Sher** (Martin Glass).

*Photo: Chris Davies*

**4. Cyrano de Bergerac (1983)** by Edmond Rostand in a new translation by Anthony Burgess. Directed by **Terry Hands** and designed by Ralph Koltai, it went, with *Much Ado About Nothing,* to Los Angeles, New York and Washington.

**Pete Postlethwaite** (Ragueneau), **Alice Krige** (Roxane), **Derek Jacobi** (Cyrano), **John Bowe** (Le Bret).

# AFTERWORD
# TREVOR NUNN

We live at a time when history is old newsreels, and when changes in our culture can be reassessed on gramophone records and moving pictures. Great film stars grown old watch themselves caught, like the figures on Keats' Grecian urn, forever young and beautiful, and it will soon be commonplace to video not only your wedding and your graduation or barmitzvah, but the birth of your child. So it's tempting to feel, surrounded as we are by photographic technology of every kind at every moment of our lives, that every experience is recoverable — even a theatre performance.

The performance of Burbage and Garrick, Siddons and Terry live on in the memory (and in the occasional stylised etching) and time, and perhaps some hyperbole from excited diarists, lent their achievements a sense of something legendary and enduring beyond the changes of fickle fashion. Nowadays we know from photographs and television recordings *exactly* what an actor's performance looked like: the wig, the costume, the make-up, the surrounding set and lighting, and so we might have the feeling that the theatre is ephemeral no more. But it isn't so.

Micheline Steinberg has researched this book with great love, enthusiasm and care, but I am sure she would be the first to agree that no publication can improve on or detract from those *remembered* moments when theatrical magic has worked.

Some readers may feel that their memories are actually contradicted by the pictorial history in these pages. Gentle reader please do not adjust your memory! The field of long grass where I played as a child was as big to me then as a prairie, and as high as an elephant's eye. When I look at it now I see it was half an acre of overgrown wasteland — but my memory is more real than the fact! Because the theatre is a living phenomenon, and because it depends upon the imagination of the audience, its effect is in the mind, and on the spirit; it has the power to change people in ways that cannot always be recorded.

There are two layers of subtext to this history, which appears as we celebrate twenty-five years of existence of the RSC in Stratford and London. Our Company has maintained a higher output of productions than any other company in the world throughout this time. The majority of this extraordinary variety of work has been achieved by a relatively small group of associate directors and designers who have remained a constant during this period of development and expansion. With the exception of Sir Peter Hall, who left to accept the task of leading the National Theatre of Great Britain, and who yet remains a consultant of the RSC, no director nominated as an associate has ever left that group either in practice or in spirit. This book records in chapters 6 and 7 a period (most of *my* working lifetime, so I can offer it in lieu of memoirs) of *shared* effort, *shared* falterings and *shared* triumphs. It records continuity, not only in direction and design, but in the identity of a group of leading actors whose loyalty to and sacrifice for the ensemble ideal has been inspirational.

Secondly, everything discussed and pictured in the account of the Company work from 1962 onwards was in one way or another subsidised. The RSC has been able to perform an unprecedented range of work, on a multiplicity of stages, to an every increasing nationwide audience because of the principle of subsidy. Without subsidy, the Company would have remained seasonal, festival, and incapable of the continuity which has been the primary factor in its development.

By the end of this century, these photographs will have faded still more and the styles of presentation and appearance will look increasingly quaint. But because the RSC has a sense of history and a sense of purpose, it must be recorded in this volume that if the provision of subsidy to the theatre in this country is, in the minds of government, to be gradually eliminated, the book recording the next period of our work will be brief and sad and shameful.

But for now, let us celebrate the past.

# Index of Names

# Index of Titles

Photographers whose work appears in this book are
*Tony Armstrong Jones, Anthony, Sophie Baker, Laurence Burns, Nobby Clark, Joe Cocks, Donald Cooper, Daniels, Chris Davies, Zoë Dominic, Downey, Foulsham & Banfield, Gordon Goode, Claude Harris, Erich Hartmann-Hangmun, John Haynes, Tom Holte, Douglas Jeffery, Jerome Ltd, Alastair Muir, Angus McBean, McLanachan, Morris Newcombe, Robert Pascall, Philip Sayer, David Sim, C.W. Smartt, J Styles, John Timbers, Topix, Mark Williamson, Reg Wilson, George Xanthos,* and the unknown photographers whose pictures appear in the earlier chapters.